Parametric Modeling

with Pro/ENGINEER

Randy H. Shih
Oregon Institute of Technology

PUBLICATIONS

Schroff Development Corporation

Mission, Kansas

Schroff Development Corporation

P.O. Box 1334

Mission KS 66222

(913) 262-2664

www.schroff.com

Shih, Randy H.
        Parametric modeling with Pro/ENGINEER 2001/
Randy H. Shih

        ISBN 1-58503-026-0

Printed and bound in the United States of America.

Preface

The primary goal of *Parametric Modeling with Pro/ENGINEER* is to introduce the aspects of **Solid Modeling** and **Parametric Modeling**. This text is intended to be used as a training guide for students and professionals. This text covers Pro/ENGINEER and the lessons proceed in a pedagogical fashion to guide you from constructing basic shapes to building intelligent solid models and creating multi-view drawings. This text takes a hands-on, exercise-intensive approach to all the important *Parametric Modeling* techniques and concepts. This textbook contains a series of ten tutorial style lessons designed to introduce beginning CAD users to Pro/ENGINEER. This text is also helpful to Pro/ENGINEER users upgrading from a previous release of the software. The solid modeling techniques and concepts discussed in this text are also applicable to other parametric feature-based CAD packages. The basic premise of this book is that the more designs you create using Pro/ENGINEER, the better you learn the software. With this in mind, each lesson introduces a new set of commands and concepts, building on previous lessons. This book does not attempt to cover all of the Pro/ENGINEER's features, only to provide an introduction to the software. It is intended to help you establish a good basis for exploring and growing in the exciting field of **Computer Aided Engineering**.

Acknowledgments

This book would not have been possible without a great deal of support. First, special thanks to two great teachers, Prof. George R. Schade of University of Nebraska-Lincoln and Mr. Denwu Lee, who taught me the fundamentals, the intrigue, and the sheer fun of Computer Aided Engineering.

The effort and support of the editorial and production staff of Schroff Development Corporation is gratefully acknowledged. I would especially like to thank Stephen Schroff and Mary Schmidt for their support and helpful suggestions during this project.

I am grateful that the Mechanical Engineering Technology Department of Oregon Institute of Technology has provided me with an excellent environment in which to pursue my interests in teaching and research.

Finally, truly unbounded thanks are due to my wife Hsiu-Ling and our daughter Casandra for their understanding and encouragement throughout this project.

Randy H. Shih
Klamath Falls, Oregon

Table of Contents

Preface
Acknowledgments

Introduction

Lesson 1
Parametric Modeling Fundamentals

Lesson 2
Constructive Solid Geometry Concepts

Lesson 3
Model History Tree

Lesson 4
Parent/Child Relationships

Lesson 5
Parametric Relations

Lesson 6
Geometric Constraints

Lesson 7
Symmetrical Features in Designs

Lesson 8
Three Dimensional Construction Tools

Lesson 9
Advanced Modeling Tools

Lesson 10
Assembly – Putting It All Together

INDEX

Notes:

Introduction

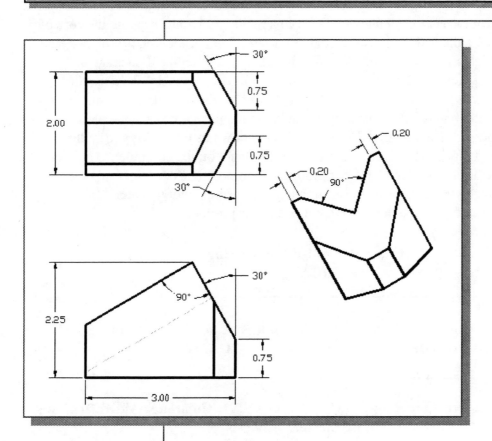

Learning Objectives

- ◆ **Development of Computer Geometric Modeling**
- ◆ **Feature-Based Parametric Modeling**
- ◆ **Getting Started with Pro/ENGINEER**
- ◆ **Startup Options and Units Setup**
- ◆ **Pro/ENGINEER Screen Layout**
- ◆ **Mouse Buttons**
- ◆ **Pro/ENGINEER On-Line Help**

Introduction

The rapid changes in the field of **Computer Aided Engineering** (CAE) have brought exciting advances in the engineering community. Recent advances have made the long-sought goal of **concurrent engineering** closer to a reality. CAE has become the core of concurrent engineering and is aimed at reducing design time, producing prototypes faster, and achieving higher product quality. Pro/ENGINEER is an integrated package of Mechanical Computer Aided Engineering software tools developed by *Parametric Technology Corporation* (**PTC**). Pro/ENGINEER is a tool that facilitates a concurrent engineering approach to the design, analysis, and manufacturing of mechanical engineering products. The Pro/ENGINEER software allows us to quickly create three-dimensional solid models. Real-life loads can be simulated on the computer to predict the behaviors of the designs under specific operating conditions. The computer models can also be used directly by manufacturing equipment such as machining centers, lathes, mills, or rapid prototyping machines to manufacture the product.

Computer Aided Engineering
(CAE)

Computer Aided Design   **Computer Aided Manufacturing**
(CAD)   **(CAM)**

Computer Geometric Modeling   **Computer Aided Drafting**
Finite Element Analysis

Development of Computer Geometric Modeling

Computer geometric modeling is a relatively new technology and its rapid expansion in the last fifty years is truly amazing. Computer-modeling technology advanced along with the development of computer hardware. The first generation CAD programs, developed in the 1950s, were mostly non-interactive; CAD users were required to create program-codes to generate the desired two-dimensional (2D) geometric shapes. Initially, the development of CAD technology occurred mostly in academic research facilities. The Massachusetts Institute of Technology, Carnegie-Mellon University, and Cambridge University were the lead pioneers at that time. The interest in CAD technology spread quickly and several major industry companies, such as General Motors, Lockheed, McDonnell, IBM, and Ford Motor Co., participated in the development of interactive CAD programs in the 1960s. Usage of CAD systems was primarily in the automotive industry, aerospace industry, and government agencies that developed their own programs for their specific needs. The 1960s also marked the beginning of the development of finite element analysis methods for computer stress analysis and computer aided manufacturing for generating machine toolpaths.

The 1970s are generally viewed as the years of the most significant progress in the development of computer hardware, namely the invention and development of **microprocessors**. With the improvement in computing power, new types of 3D CAD programs that were user-friendly and interactive became reality. CAD technology quickly expanded from very simple **computer aided drafting** to very complex **computer aided design**. The use of 2D and 3D wireframe modelers was accepted as the leading edge technology that could increase productivity in industry. The developments of surface modeling and solid modeling technology were taking shape by the late 1970s; but the high cost of computer hardware and programming slowed the development of such technology. During this time period, the available CAD systems all required expensive room-sized mainframe computers that were extremely high in cost.

In the 1980s, improvements in computer hardware brought the power of mainframes to the desktop at less cost and with more accessibility to the general public. By the mid-1980s, CAD technology had become the main focus of a variety of manufacturing industries and was very competitive with traditional design/drafting methods. It was during this period of time that 3D solid modeling technology had major advancements, which boosted the usage of CAE technology in industry.

The introduction of the *feature-based parametric solid modeling* approach, at the end of the 1980s, elevated CAD/CAM/CAE technology to a new level. In the 1990s, CAD programs evolved into powerful design/manufacturing/management tools. CAD technology has come a long way, and during these years of development, modeling schemes progressed from two-dimensional (2D) wireframe to three-dimensional (3D) wireframe, to surface modeling, to solid modeling and, finally, to feature-based parametric solid modeling.

The first generation CAD packages were simply 2D **Computer Aided Drafting** programs, basically the electronic equivalents of the drafting board. For typical models, the use of this type of program would require that several to many views of the objects be created individually as they would be on the drafting board. The 3D designs remained in the designer's mind, not in the computer database. The mental translation of 3D objects to 2D views is required throughout the use of the packages. Although such systems have some advantages over traditional board drafting, they are still tedious and labor intensive. The need for the development of 3D modelers came quite naturally, given the limitations of the 2D drafting packages.

The development of three-dimensional modeling schemes started with three-dimensional (3D) wireframes. Wireframe models are models consisting of points and edges, which are straight lines connecting between appropriate points. The edges of wireframe models are used, similar to lines in 2D drawings, to represent transitions of surfaces and features. The use of lines and points is also a very economical way to represent 3D designs.

The development of the 3D wireframe modeler was a major leap in the area of computer geometric modeling. The computer database in the 3D wireframe modeler contains the locations of all the points in space coordinates and it is typically sufficient to create just one model rather than multiple views of the same model. This single 3D model can then be viewed from any direction as needed. Most 3D wireframe modelers allow the user to create projected lines/edges of 3D wireframe models. In comparison to other types of 3D modelers, 3D wireframe modelers require very little computing power and generally can be used to achieve reasonably good representations of 3D models. However, because surface definition is not part of a wireframe model, all wireframe images have the inherent problem of ambiguity. Two examples of such ambiguity are illustrated.

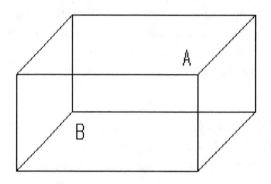

Wireframe Ambiguity: Which corner is in front, A or B?

A non-realizable object: Wireframe models contain no surface definitions.

Surface modeling is the logical development in computer geometry modeling to follow the 3D wireframe modeling scheme by organizing and grouping edges that define polygonal surfaces. Surface modeling describes the part's surfaces but not its interiors. Designers are still required to interactively examine surface models to insure that the various surfaces on a model are contiguous throughout. Many of the concepts used in 3D wireframe and surface modelers are incorporated in the solid modeling scheme, but it is solid modeling that offers the most advantages as a design tool.

In the solid modeling presentation scheme, the solid definitions include nodes, edges, and surfaces, and it is a complete and unambiguous mathematical representation of a precisely enclosed and filled volume. Unlike the surface modeling method, solid modelers start with a solid or use topology rules to guarantee that all of the surfaces are stitched together properly. Two predominant methods for representing solid models are **constructive solid geometry** (CSG) representation and **boundary representation** (B-rep).

The CSG representation method can be defined as the combination of 3D solid primitives. What constitutes a "primitive" varies somewhat with the software but typically includes a rectangular prism, a cylinder, a cone, a wedge, and a sphere. Most solid modelers also allow the user to define additional primitives, which are shapes typically formed by the basic shapes. The underlying concept of the CSG representation method is very straightforward; we simply **add** or **subtract** one primitive from another. The CSG approach is also known as the machinist's approach as it can be used to simulate the manufacturing procedures for creating the 3D object.

In the B-rep representation method, objects are represented in terms of their spatial boundaries. This method defines the points, edges, and surfaces of a volume, and/or issues commands that sweep or rotate a defined face into a third dimension to form a solid. The object is then made up of the unions of these surfaces that completely and precisely enclose a volume.

By the 1980s, a new paradigm called *concurrent engineering* had emerged. With concurrent engineering, designers, design engineers, analysts, manufacturing engineers, and management engineers all work closely together right from the initial stages of the design. In this way, all aspects of the design can be evaluated and any potential problems can be identified right from the start and throughout the design process. Using the principles of concurrent engineering, a new type of computer modeling technique appeared. The technique is known as the *feature-based parametric modeling technique*. The key advantage of the feature-based parametric modeling technique is its capability to produce very flexible designs. Changes can be made easily and design alternatives can be evaluated with minimum effort. Various software packages offer different approaches to feature-based parametric modeling, yet the end result is a flexible design defined by its design variables and parametric features.

Feature-Based Parametric Modeling

One of the key-elements in the *Pro/ENGINEER* solid modeling software is its use of the **feature-based parametric modeling technique**. The feature-based parametric modeling approach has elevated solid modeling technology to the level of a very powerful design tool. Parametric modeling automates design and revision procedures by the use of parametric features. Parametric features control the model geometry by the use of design variables. The word *parametric* means that the geometric definitions of the design, such as dimensions, can be varied at any time in the design process. Features are predefined parts or construction tools in which users define the key parameters. A part is described as a sequence of engineering features, which can be modified/changed at any time. The concept of parametric features makes the modeling more closely match the actual design-manufacturing process than the mathematics of a solid modeling program. In parametric modeling, models and drawings are updated automatically when the design is refined.

Parametric modeling offers many benefits:

- **We begin with simple, conceptual models with minimal detail; this approach conforms to the design philosophy of "shape before size."**

- **Geometric constraints, dimensional constraints, and relational parametric equations can be used to capture design intent.**

- **The ability to update an entire system, including parts, assemblies and drawings after changing one parameter of complex designs.**

- **We can quickly explore and evaluate different design variations and alternatives to determine the best design.**

- **Existing design data can be reused to create new designs.**

- **Quick design turn-around.**

The feature-based parametric modeling technique enables the designer to incorporate the original **design intent** into the construction of the model, and the individual features control the geometry in the event of a design change. As features are modified, the system updates the entire part by re-linking the individual features of the model.

Pro/ENGINEER 2001 is the twenty-third release, with many added features and enhancements, of the original *Pro/ENGINEER* software produced by Parametric Technology Corporation (PTC). *Pro/ENGINEER* is considered the industry leader in setting the standard for the feature-based modeling paradigm. *Pro/ENGINEER's* **Behavioral Modeling** and **Intent Referencing** allow users to concentrate on the design without depending on the associated parameters or constraints. Users can specify how features interact with each other and *Pro/ENGINEER* will automatically adjust sizes and positions as changes are made.

Getting Started with *Pro/ENGINEER*

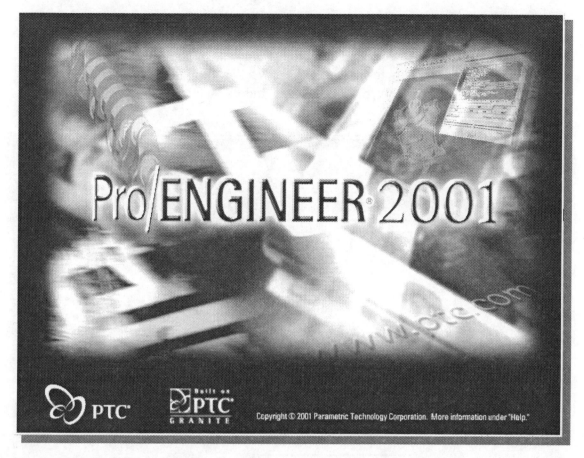

- *Pro/ENGINEER* is composed of several application software modules (these modules are called *applications*), all sharing a common database. In this text, the main concentration is placed on the solid modeling modules used for part design. The general procedures required in creating solid models, engineering drawings, and assemblies are illustrated.

Starting *Pro/ENGINEER*

How to start *Pro/ENGINEER* depends on the type of workstation and the particular software configuration you are using. With most *Windows* and *UNIX* systems, you may select **Pro/ENGINEER** on the *Start* menu or select the **Pro/ENGINEER** icon on the desktop. Consult your instructor or technical support personnel if you have difficulty starting the software.

The program takes a while to load, so be patient. The tutorials in this text are based on the assumption that you are using *Pro/ENGINEER's* default settings. If your system has been customized for other uses, some of the settings may appear differently and not work with the step-by-step instructions in the tutorials. Contact your instructor and/or technical support personnel to restore the default software configuration.

Pro/ENGINEER Screen Layout

The default *Pro/ENGINEER drawing screen* contains the *pull-down menus*, the *Standard* toolbar, the *message area*, the *graphics display area*, the *Datum* toolbar and the *single line Help*. A line of quick text appears next to the icon as you move the *mouse cursor* over different icons. You may resize the *Pro/ENGINEER* drawing window by click and drag at the edges of the window, or relocate the window by click and drag at the window title area.

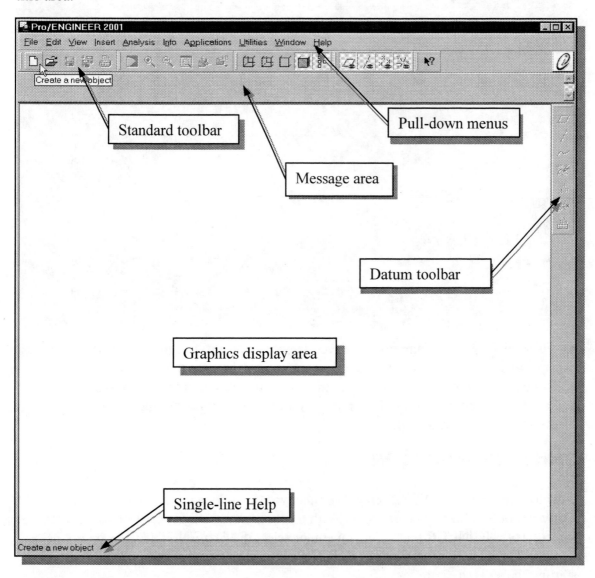

Pro/ENGINEER uses the **context sensitive menus** approach, which means additional selection menus and option windows will only be available when they are applicable to the current task. The appearance of the *Pro/ENGINEER* main window and toolbars, as shown in the figure above, remains the same on the screen throughout the different phases of modeling. Note that the menu items and icons of the non-applicable options are grayed out, which means they are temporarily disabled.

- **Pull-down menus**

  The pull-down menus at the top of the main window contain operations that you can use for all modes of the system. Note that the quick key combination to activate the same command is also shown in the displayed pull-down list.

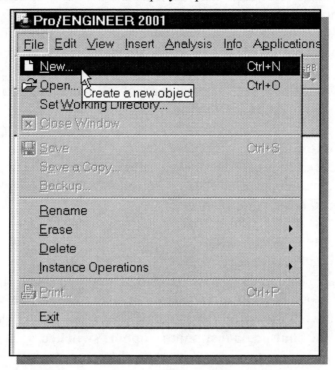

- **Standard toolbar**

  The *Standard* toolbar located at the top of the main window, below the pull-down menus, allows us quick access to frequently used commands. For example, the *view related* commands, such as **Zoom**, **Pan**, and **Shaded Image**, are tools to help manipulate the viewing of graphical objects. We can customize the toolbar by adding and removing sets of options or individual commands.

- **Message area**

  The section below of the *Standard* toolbar provides status information for an operation and it is also the area for data input.

- **Graphics display area**

  The graphics display area is the area where parts, assemblies, and drawings are displayed. The model's display is controlled by the *environment settings*.

- **Datum toolbar**

  The *Datum* toolbar, located toward the right section of the main window, provides us with quick access to create datum references such as datum planes and datum axes.

Mouse Buttons

Pro/ENGINEER utilizes the mouse buttons extensively. In learning *Pro/ENGINEER's* interactive environment, it is important to understand the basic functions of the mouse buttons. It is highly recommended that you use a three-button mouse with *Pro/ENGINEER* since the package uses all three buttons for various functions. If you are using a two-button mouse, you will need to switch ***on*** the *Pro/ENGINEER* two-button mouse support option, the user preference option: **2button_mouse_mmb_support**. Otherwise, you will not be able to perform some of the operations such as the *Dynamic Rotate* function.

- **Left mouse button**
  The left mouse button is used for most operations, such as selecting menus and icons, or picking graphic entities. One click of the button is used to select icons, menus and form entries, and to pick graphic items.

- **Middle mouse button**
  The middle button is often used to accept the default setting of a prompt or to end a process. It is also used in the *Pro/ENGINEER Sketcher* to create circles and place dimensions. **If you are using a two-button mouse, you can hold down the SHIFT key and use the left mouse button to get the same result as clicking the middle button (with the 2button_mouse_mmb_support switched *on*.)**

- **Right mouse button**
  The right mouse button is used to query a selection, and is also used in the *Pro/ENGINEER Sketcher* to create tangent arcs.

Accepts the default option of a command, or ends a process. **For a two-button mouse, hold down the SHIFT key and click with the left-mouse-button to emulate the middle-mouse-button.**

Brings up additional available options.

Picks icons, menus and graphic entities.

Model Tree window and Menu Manager

❖ The *Pro/ENGINEER **Model Tree*** window and ***Menu Manager*** are two of the most important *Pro/ENGINEER* interfaces; they will appear on the screen when we begin a modeling session.

1. Click on the **New** icon, located in the *Standard* toolbar as shown.

2. In the *New* dialogue box, confirm the model's **Type** is set to **Part** (and the **Sub-type** is set to **Solid**).

3. Click on the **OK** button to accept the default settings and enter the *Pro/ENGINEER Part Modeling* mode.

❖ Note the ***Model Tree*** and the ***Menu Manager*** appear on the screen as shown below.

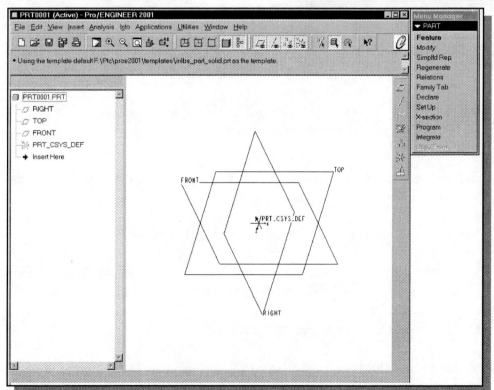

Customize the Pro/E Screen Layout

❖ As a general rule, one should adjust the working environment to meet one's individual needs. We will customize the screen layout by changing the location of the message area and the settings of the *Model Tree* window to maximize the graphics area.

1. Click on **Utilities** at the top of the *Pro/ENGINEER* main window, and then choose **Customize Screen** from the pulldown menu.

2. In the *Customize* dialogue box, click on the **Options** tab as shown in the below figure.

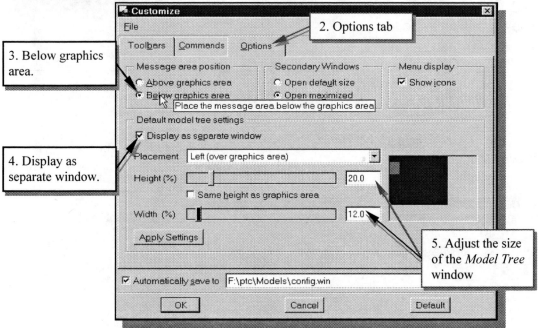

3. Set the position of the message area to be placed **below** the graphics area as shown in the above figure.

4. Set the *Model Tree* to be displayed as a **separate window**.

5. Adjust the height and width of the *Model Tree* window as shown in the above figure. (Hint: Turn *off* the **Same height as graphics area** option.)

6. Click on the **OK** button to accept the settings.

➢ Note that changes are stored in the **config.win** file of the startup directory. On your own, make a backup copy of the **config.win** file, preferably onto a floppy disk.

[Esc] - Canceling Commands

❖ The [**Esc**] key is used to cancel a command in *Pro/ENGINEER*. The [**Esc**] key is located near the top-left corner of the keyboard. Sometimes, we can also use the middle mouse button to cancel a command; it depends upon where we are in the command sequence. For some commands, the [**Esc**] key is used to exit the command.

On-Line Help

❖ Several types of on-line *Help* are available at any time during a *Pro/ENGINEER* session. *Pro/ENGINEER* provides many help functions, such as:

- *Pro/ENGINEER Help System*: Click on the **Help** option in the pull-down menus to access the many *Pro/ENGINEER* **online** *Help* **systems**.

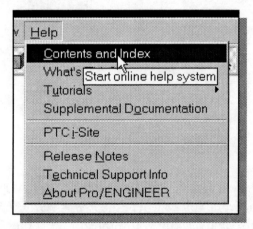

- Supplemental Documentation: Click on the **Help - Supplemental Documentation** option in the pull-down menus to access the *Pro/ENGINEER* **online books**.

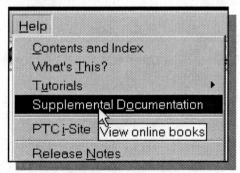

- Context Sensitive Help: The context sensitive help can be used to quickly access the **Help** menu on specific tasks or icons displayed on the screen.

Leaving *Pro/ENGINEER*

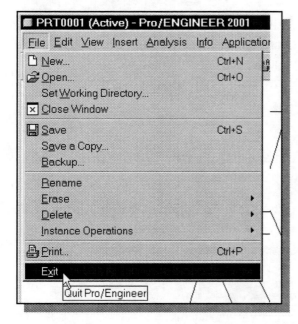

1. To leave *Pro/ENGINEER*, use the left-mouse-button and click on **File** at the top of the *Pro/ENGINEER* main window, then choose **Exit** from the pull-down menu.

2. In the confirmation dialog box, click on the **Yes** button to exit *Pro/ENGINEER*.

Creating a CAD files folder

It is a good practice to create a separate folder to store your CAD files. You should not save your CAD files in the same folder where the *Pro/ENGINEER* application is located. It is much easier to organize and backup your project files if they are in a separate folder. Making folders within this folder for different types of projects will help you organize your CAD files even further. When creating CAD files in *Pro/ENGINEER*, it is strongly recommended that you *save* your CAD files on the hard drive.

To create a new folder with most *Windows* systems:
1. In *My Computer*, or start the **Windows Explorer** under the *Start* menu, open the folder in which you want to create a new folder.

2. On the **File** menu, point to **New**, and then click **Folder**. The new folder appears with a temporary name.

3. Type a name for the new folder, and then press **ENTER**.

Lesson 1
Parametric Modeling Fundamentals

Learning Objectives

When you have completed this lesson, you will be able to:
♦ Create Simple Extruded Solid Models.
♦ Understand the Basic Parametric Modeling Process.
♦ Create 2-D Sketches.
♦ Understand the "Shape Before Size" approach.
♦ Use the Dynamic Viewing commands.
♦ Create and Modify Parametric Dimensions.

Introduction

The **feature-based parametric modeling** technique enables the designer to incorporate the original **design intent** into the construction of the model. The word *parametric* means the geometric definitions of the design, such as dimensions, can be varied at any time in the design process. Parametric modeling is accomplished by identifying and creating the key features of the design with the aid of computer software. The design variables, described in the sketches and features, can be used to quickly modify/update the design.

In *Pro/ENGINEER*, the parametric part modeling process involves the following steps:

1. **Set up Units and Basic Datum Geometry.**

2. **Determine the type of the base feature, the first solid feature, of the design. Note that *Extrude*, *Revolve*, or *Sweep* operations are the most common types of base features.**

3. **Create a rough two-dimensional sketch of the basic shape of the base feature of the design.**

4. **Apply/modify constraints and dimensions to the two-dimensional sketch.**

5. **Transform the parametric two-dimensional sketch into a 3D solid.**

6. **Add additional parametric features by identifying feature relations and complete the design.**

7. **Perform analyses/simulations, such as finite element analysis (FEA) or cutter path generation (CNC), on the computer model and refine the design as needed.**

8. **Document the design by creating the desired 2D/3D drawings.**

The approach of creating three-dimensional features using two-dimensional sketches is an effective way to construct solid models. Many designs are in fact the same shape in one direction. Computer input and output devices we use today are largely two-dimensional in nature, which makes this modeling technique quite practical. This method also conforms to the design process that helps the designer with conceptual design along with the capability to capture the *design intent*. Most engineers and designers can relate to the experience of making rough sketches on restaurant napkins to convey conceptual design ideas. Note that *Pro/ENGINEER* provides many powerful modeling and design tools, and there are many different approaches to accomplish modeling tasks. The basic principle of **feature-based modeling** is to build models by adding simple features one at a time. In this chapter, a very simple solid model with extruded features is used to introduce the general **feature-based parametric** modeling procedure.

The *Adjuster* design

Starting *Pro/ENGINEER*

How to start *Pro/ENGINEER* depends on the type of workstation and the particular software configuration you are using. With most *Windows* and *UNIX* systems, you may select **Pro/ENGINEER** on the *Start* menu or select the **Pro/ENGINEER** icon on the desktop. Consult your instructor or technical support personnel if you have difficulty starting the software.

1. Select the **Pro/ENGINEER** option on the *Start* menu or select the **Pro/ENGINEER** icon on the desktop to start *Pro/ENGINEER*. The *Pro/ENGINEER* main window will appear on the screen.

2. Click on the **New** icon, located in the *Standard* toolbar as shown.

3. In the *New* dialogue box, confirm the model's **Type** is set to **Part** (**Solid** Sub-type).

4. Enter **Adjuster** as the part **Name** as shown in the figure.

5. Turn *off* the **Use default template** option.

6. Click on the **OK** button to accept the settings.

7. In the *New File Options* dialogue box, select **EMPTY** in the option list to not use any template file.

8. Click on the **OK** button to accept the settings and enter the *Pro/ENGINEER Part Modeling* mode.

❖ Note that the part name, *Adjuster*, appears in the title area of the main window and in the *Model Tree* window.

➢ If the *Pro/ENGINEER* screen layout appeared differently on your screen, open the saved **config.win** file to adjust the screen layout to the customized screen layout outlined on page **Intro-12**:

Utilities → Customize Screen
→ File → Open Settings
→ config.win   (If necessary, change directory to locate the file.)

Step 1: Units and Basic Datum Geometry Setups

♦ Units Setup and *Pro/ENGINEER* Menu Structure

When starting a new model, the first thing we should do is to choose the set of units we want to use.

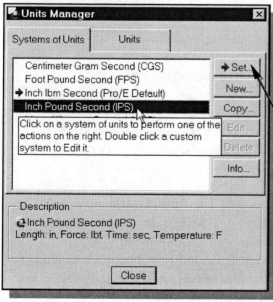

1. Use the left-mouse-button and select **Set Up** in the **Menu Manager** window. In the **Menu Manager** window, the **Set Up** submenu is displayed underneath the **PART** menu. The *Pro/ENGINEER* menu system uses a **tree structure**; we start at the root and follow the branches to reach the leaves (commands).

2. Select the **Units** option. Notice that more submenu selections are displayed. A scrollbar is available as more submenus are displayed.

1. Pick **Set Up**

2. Pick **Units**

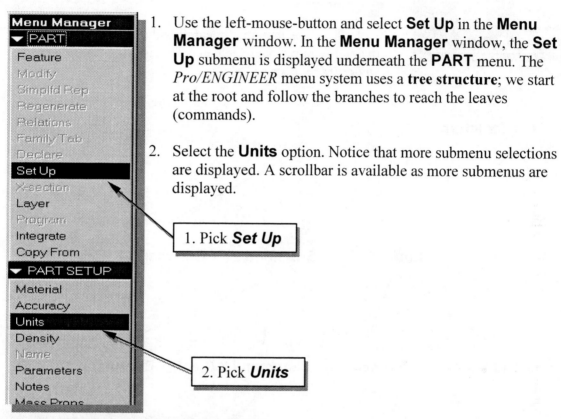

3. In the **Units Manager-System of Units** form, the *Pro/ENGINEER* default setting **Inch lbm Second** is displayed. The set of units is stored with the model file when you save. Pick **Inch Pound Second (IPS)**, by clicking in the list window as shown.

4. Pick **Set**

4. Click on the **Set** button to accept the selection.

5. In the *Warning* dialog box, click on the **OK** button to accept the change of the units.

6. Click on the **Close** button to exit the *Units Manager* dialog box.

7. Pick **Done** to exit the **PART Set Up** submenu.

7. Pick *Done*

➢ Note that the submenu appeared and disappeared as different options were selected; this is known as the *tree structure menu system*.

♦ **Tree Structure**

The tree structure is an effective way to organize menu items. Similar items are placed in a group that could belong to another subgroup based on the grouping method. The submenus represent different categories of items. The tree structure is used extensively in the majority of CAD software menu systems.

Using the tree structure shown, we will follow **Submenu 1** to **Submenu 3** and reach **Command 5**. If we then want to switch to **Command 4**, we will trace back to the root then branch off to **Submenu 2**. Keep this tree structure in mind while using the *Pro/ENGINEER* menu system. Think of the overall scheme and it will be quite easy to get to where you want to go. In *Pro/ENGINEER*, the **Done** option will usually return you to the previous level in the menu structure.

◆ Adding the First Part Features — Datum Planes

❖ *Pro/ENGINEER* provides many powerful tools for model creation. In doing feature-based parametric modeling, it is a good practice to establish three reference planes to locate the part in space. The reference planes can be used as location references in feature constructions.

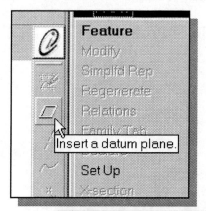

➢ Move the cursor toward the right side of the main window and click on the **Datum Plane** icon as shown.

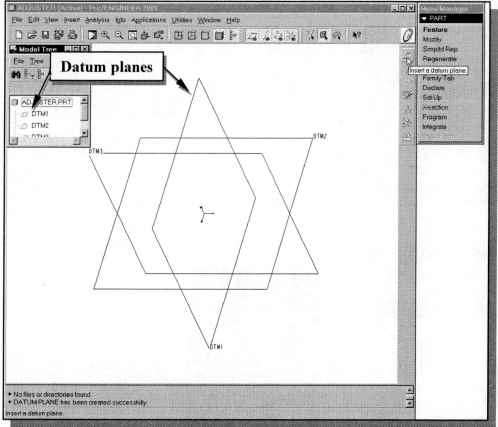

❖ In the display area, three datum planes represented by three rectangles are displayed. Datum planes are infinite planes and they are perpendicular to each other. We can consider these planes as XY, YZ, and ZX planes of a Cartesian coordinate system. Notice in the *Model Tree* window, three datum plane features are added to the tree structure.

Step 2: Determine/Set Up the Base Solid Feature

- For the *Adjuster* design, we will create an extruded solid as the base feature.

1. In the **Menu Manager** window, select

   Feature → Create → Solid → Protrusion

   1. Pick *Feature*

   2. Pick *Create*

   3. Pick *Solid*

   4. Pick *Protrusion*

2. In the **SOLID OPTS** submenu, select

   Extrude → Solid → Done

   Select

- The protrusion's feature dialog box appears on the screen. We will need to define all the elements listed to complete the feature.

3. In the **ATTRIBUTES** submenu, select

   One Side → Done

Sketching plane – It is an XY CRT, but an XYZ World

Design modeling software is becoming more powerful and user friendly, yet the system still does only what the user tells it to do. When using a geometric modeler, we therefore need to have a good understanding of what its inherent limitations are. We should also have a good understanding of what we want to do and what to expect, as the results are based on what is available.

In most 3D geometric modelers, 3D objects are located and defined in what is usually called **world space** or **global space**. Although a number of different coordinate systems can be used to create and manipulate objects in a 3D modeling system, the objects are typically defined and stored using the world space. The world space is usually a **3D Cartesian coordinate system** that the user cannot change or manipulate.

In most engineering designs, models can be very complex, and it would be tedious and confusing if only the world coordinate system were available. Practical 3D modeling systems allow the user to define **Local Coordinate Systems (LCS)** or **User Coordinate Systems (UCS)** relative to the world coordinate system. Once a local coordinate system is defined, we can then create geometry in terms of this more convenient system.

Although objects are created and stored in 3D space coordinates, most of the geometric entities can be referenced using 2D Cartesian coordinate systems. Typical input devices such as a mouse or digitizer are two-dimensional by nature; the movement of the input device is interpreted by the system in a planar sense. The same limitation is true of common output devices, such as CRT displays and plotters. The modeling software performs a series of three-dimensional to two-dimensional transformations to correctly project 3D objects onto the 2D display plane.

The *Pro/ENGINEER* **sketching plane** is a special construction approach that enables the planar nature of the 2D input devices to be directly mapped into the 3D coordinate system. The *sketching plane* is a local coordinate system that can be aligned to an existing face of a part, or a reference plane.

Think of the sketching plane as the surface on which we can sketch the 2D sections of the parts. It is similar to a piece of paper, a white board, or a chalkboard that can be attached to any planar surface. The first sketch we create is usually drawn on one of the established datum planes. Subsequent sketches/features can then be created on sketching planes that are aligned to existing **planar faces of the solid part** or **datum planes.**

Defining the Sketching Plane

1. The *sketching plane* is a reference location where we create the two-dimensional sketch. The *sketching plane* can be any planar part surface or datum plane. We will use *datum plane* **DTM2** as the sketching plane. Pick **DTM2** by clicking the left-mouse-button on either the edge or the nametag of the datum plane.

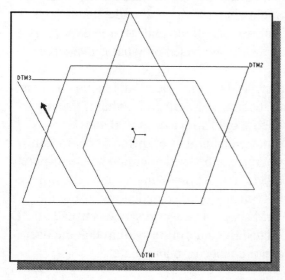

2. A red arrow appears on the edge of **DTM2**, and the message "*Arrow shows direction of feature creation. Pick Flip or Okay.*" is displayed in the message area. The arrow direction indicates the direction of the feature we are creating. In this case, it is the **direction of extrusion.** Confirm the arrow is pointing upward from **DTM2** as shown in the figure.

3. In the **DIRECTION** submenu, pick **Okay** to accept the selection of the sketching plane.

Pick *Okay*

Defining the Orientation of the Sketching Plane

- Although we have selected the sketching plane, *Pro/ENGINEER* still needs additional information to define the orientation of the part with respect to the other two planes. *Pro/ENGINEER* asks us to define a reference plane relative to the computer screen.

❏ **To define the orientation of the sketching plane, select the facing direction of the reference plane with respect to the computer screen.**

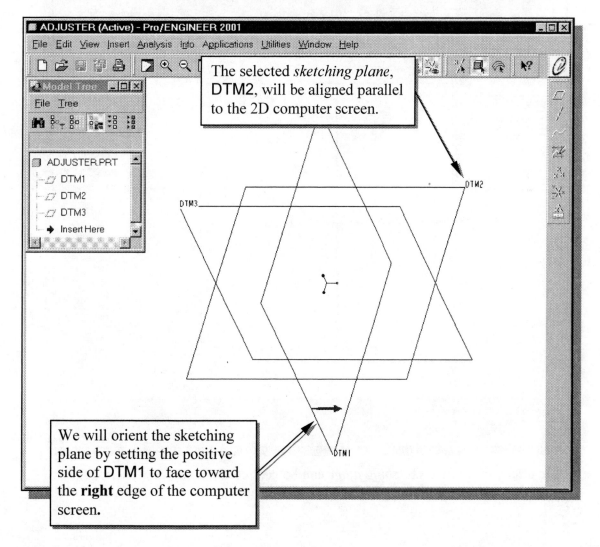

The selected *sketching plane*, DTM2, will be aligned parallel to the 2D computer screen.

We will orient the sketching plane by setting the positive side of DTM1 to face toward the **right** edge of the computer screen.

1. In the **SKET VIEW** submenu, pick **Right**.

2. In the display area, pick the positive side (yellow side) of **DTM1**.

1. Pick *Right*

3. Pick **Close** to exit the *Sketcher Enhancement* form, which provides general improvement information of the *Pro/ENGINEER Intent Manager*.

• *Pro/ENGINEER* will now rotate the three *datum planes*: **DTM2** aligned to the screen and the positive side of **DTM1** facing toward the right edge of the computer screen.

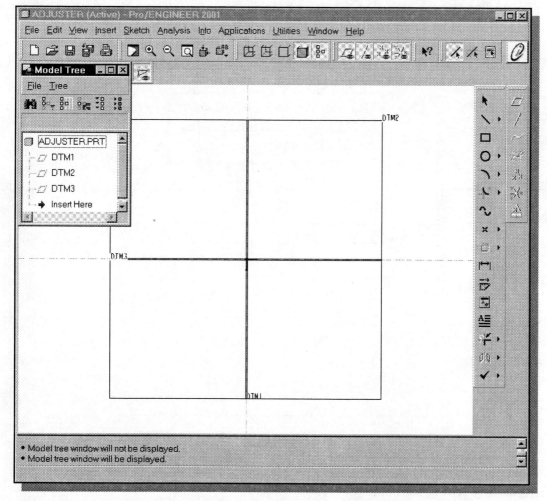

❑   The orientation of the *sketching plane* can be very confusing to new users. It is strongly recommended that you read this section again.

Step 3: Creating 2D rough sketches

♦ Shape Before Size – Creating Rough Sketches

Quite often during the early design stage, the shape of a design may not have any precise dimensions. Most conventional CAD systems require the user to input the precise lengths and location dimensions of all geometric entities defining the design, and some of the values may not be available during the early design stage. With *parametric modeling*, we can use the computer to elaborate and formulate the design idea further during the initial design stage. With *Pro/ENGINEER*, we can use the computer as an electronic sketchpad to help us concentrate on the formulation of forms and shapes for the design. This approach is the main advantage of *parametric modeling* over conventional solid-modeling techniques.

As the name implies, ***rough sketches*** are not precise at all. When sketching, we simply sketch the geometry so it closely resembles the desired shape. Precise scale or dimensions are not needed. *Pro/ENGINEER* provides us with many tools to assist in finalizing sketches, known as ***sections***. For example, geometric entities such as horizontal and vertical lines are set automatically. However, if the rough sketches are poor, much more work will be required to generate the desired parametric sketches. Here are some general guidelines for creating sketches in *Pro/ENGINEER*:

- **Create a sketch that is proportional to the desired shape.** Concentrate on the shapes and forms of the design.

- **Keep the sketches simple.** Leave out small geometry features such as fillets, rounds, and chamfers. They can easily be placed using the Fillet and Chamfer commands after the parametric sketches have been established.

- **Exaggerate the geometric features of the desired shape.** For example, if the desired angle is 85 degrees, create an angle that is 50 or 60 degrees. Otherwise, Pro/ENGINEER might assume the intended angle to be a 90-degree angle.

- **Draw the geometry so that it does not overlap.** The sketched geometry should eventually form a closed region. *Self-intersecting* geometric shapes are not allowed.

- **The sketched geometric entities should form a closed region.** To create a solid feature, such as an extruded solid, a closed region section is required so that the extruded solid forms a 3D volume.

- ➢ **Note:** The concepts and principles involved in *parametric modeling* are very different, and sometimes they are totally opposite, to those of the conventional computer aided drafting systems. In order to understand and fully utilize *Pro/ENGINEER's* functionality, it will be helpful to take a *Zen* approach to learning the topics presented in this text: **Temporarily forget your knowledge and experiences using conventional computer aided drafting systems.**

♦ The Pro/ENGINEER SKETCHER and INTENT MANAGER

In previous generation CAD programs, construction of models relies on exact dimensional values, and adjustments to dimensional values are quite difficult once the model is built. With *Pro/ENGINEER*, we can now treat the sketch as if it is being done on a napkin, and it is the general shape of the design that we are more interested in defining. The *Pro/ENGINEER* part model contains more than just the final geometry. It also contains the *design intent* that governs what will happen when geometry changes. The design philosophy of "**shape before size**" is implemented through the use of the *Pro/ENGINEER Sketcher*. This allows the designer to construct solid models in a higher level and leave all the geometric details to *Pro/ENGINEER*.

One of the main improvements in *Pro/ENGINEER* since **Release 20** is the introduction and enhancements of the *Intent Manager* in the *Pro/ENGINEER Sketcher*.

The *Intent Manager* enables us to do:
- Dynamic dimensioning and constraints
- Add or delete constraints explicitly
- Undo any *Sketcher* operation

The first thing that *Pro/ENGINEER Sketcher* expects us to do, which is displayed in the *References* window, is to specify **sketching references**. In the previous sections, we created the three datum planes to help orient the model in 3D space. Now we need to orient the 2D sketch with respect to the three datum planes. At least two references are required to orient the sketch in the horizontal direction and in the vertical direction. By default, the two planes (in our example, DTM1 and DTM3) that are perpendicular to the sketching plane (DTM2) are automatically selected.

1. Note that **DTM1** and **DTM3** are pre-selected as the sketching references. In the graphics area, the two references are highlighted and displayed with two dashed lines.

➤ The *Reference status*, as shown in the *References* dialog box, indicates the 2D sketch can be *Fully Placed* with the two references identified. We can proceed to creating 2D sketches. Click on the **Close** button to close the *References* dialog box.

❖ Next, we will create a rough sketch by using some of the visual aids available, and then update the design through the associated control parameters.

2. Move the graphics cursor to the **Line** icon in the *Sketcher* toolbar. A *help-tip* box appears next to the cursor and a brief description of the command options is displayed in the message area.

❖ The *Sketcher* toolbar, located on the right side of the main window, provides tools for creating the basic 2D geometry that can be used to create features and parts.

Graphics Cursors

❖ Notice the cursor changes from an arrow to an arrow with a small crosshair when graphical input is expected.

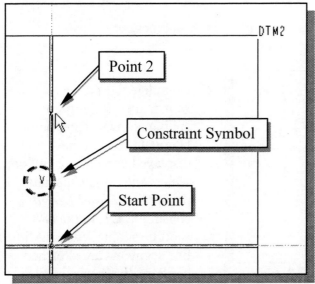

3. Move the cursor near the intersection of the two references, and notice that the small crosshair attached to the cursor will automatically snap to the intersection point. **Left-click** once to place the starting point as shown.

4. As you move the graphics cursor, you will see different symbols appear at different locations.

5. Move the cursor along the vertical reference and create a vertical line by clicking at a location above the start point (***Point 2***) as shown. Notice the geometric constraint symbol, **V**, indicating the created line is vertical.

Geometric Constraint Symbols

❖ *Pro/ENGINEER* displays different visual clues, or symbols, to show you alignments, perpendicularities, tangencies, etc. These constraints are used to capture the *design intent* by creating constraints where they are recognized. *Pro/ENGINEER* displays the governing geometric rules as models are built.

V	Vertical	indicates a segment is vertical
H	Horizontal	indicates a segment is horizontal
L	Equal Length	indicates two segments are of equal length
R	Equal Radii	indicates two curves are of equal radii
T	Tangent	indicates two entities are tangent to each other
╲╲	Parallel	indicates a segment is parallel to other entities
╲╱	Perpendicular	indicates a segment is perpendicular to other entities
→ ←	Symmetry	indicates two points are symmetrical
O	Point on Entity	indicates the point is on another entity

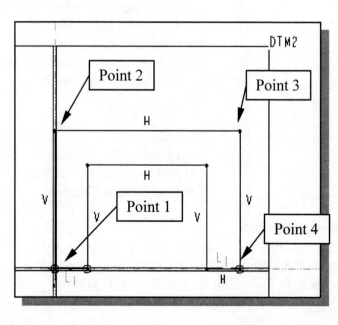

6. Complete the sketch as shown, a closed region ending at the starting point (***Point 1***). Watch the displayed constraint symbols while sketching, especially the applied ***Equal Length*** constraint, **L1**, to the two short horizontal edges. All line segments are sketched horizontally or vertically.

7. Inside the graphics area, click once with the **middle-mouse-button** to end the current line sketch.

❖ *Pro/ENGINEER's* ***Intent Manager*** automatically places dimensions and constraints on the sketched geometry. This is known as the ***Dynamic Dimensioning and Constraints*** feature. Constraints and dimensions are added "on the fly." Do not be concerned with the size of the sketched geometry or the displayed dimensional values; we will modify the sketched geometry in the following sections.

Dynamic Viewing Functions

❖ *Pro/ENGINEER* provides a special user interface, ***Dynamic Viewing,*** which enables convenient viewing of the entities in the display area at any time. The ***Dynamic Viewing*** functions are controlled with the **[Ctrl]** key on the keyboard and the mouse buttons.

Zooming – [Ctrl] key and [left-mouse-button]

Hold down the **[Ctrl]** key and press down the left-mouse-button in the display area. Drag the mouse vertically on the screen to adjust the scale of the display. Moving upward will reduce the scale of the display, making the entities display smaller on the screen. Moving downward will magnify the scale of the display.

Zoom   [Ctrl]   +   Left mouse button

Panning – [Ctrl] key and [right-mouse-button]

Hold down the **[Ctrl]** key and press down the right-mouse-button in the display area. Drag the mouse to pan the display. This allows you to reposition the display while maintaining the same scale factor of the display. This function acts as if you are using a video camera. You control the display by moving the mouse.

Pan   [Ctrl]   +   Right mouse button

➢ On your own, use the *Dynamic Viewing* functions to reposition and magnify the scale of the 2D sketch to the center of the screen so that it is easier to work with.

Step 4: Apply/modify constraints and dimensions

➤ As the sketch is made, *Pro/ENGINEER* automatically applies geometric constraints (such as horizontal, vertical and equal length) and dimensions to the sketched geometry. We can continue to modify the geometry, apply additional constraints and/or dimensions, or define/modify the size and location of the existing geometry. It is more than likely that some of the automatically applied dimensions may not match with the design intent we have in mind. For example, we might want to have dimensions identifying the overall-height, overall-width, and the width of the inside-cut of the design, as shown in the figures below.

1. Click on the **Dimension** icon in the *Sketcher* toolbar as shown. This command allows us to create defining dimensions.

2. Select the inside-horizontal line by left-clicking once on the line as shown.

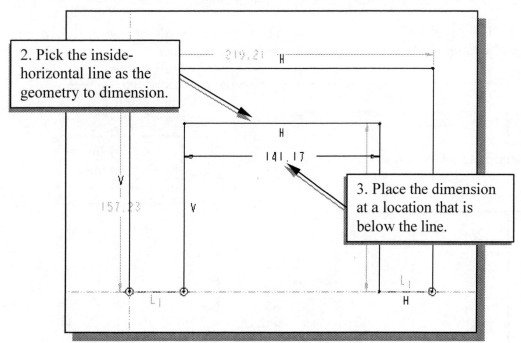

2. Pick the inside-horizontal line as the geometry to dimension.

3. Place the dimension at a location that is below the line.

3. Move the graphics cursor below the selected line and click once with the **middle-mouse-button** to place the dimension. (Note that the value displayed on your screen might be different than what is shown in the above figure.)

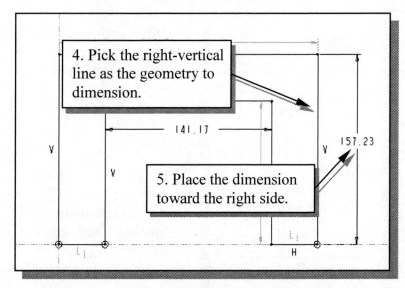

4. Pick the right-vertical line as the geometry to dimension.

5. Place the dimension toward the right side.

4. Select the right-vertical line.

5. Place the dimension, by clicking once with the **middle-mouse-button** at a location toward the right of the sketch.

❖ The **Dimension** command will create a length dimension if a single line is selected.

• Notice the overall-height dimension applied automatically by the *Intent Manager* is removed as the new dimension is defined.

❖ Note that the dimensions we just created are displayed with a different color than those that are applied automatically. The dimensions created by the *Intent Manager* are called **weak dimensions**, which can be replaced/deleted as we create specific defining dimensions to satisfy our design intent.

6. Select the top-horizontal line as shown below.

7. Select the inside-horizontal line as shown below.

8. Place the dimension, by clicking once with the **middle-mouse-button,** at a location in between the selected lines as shown below.

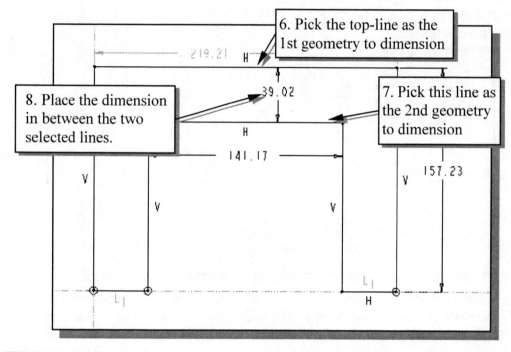

6. Pick the top-line as the 1st geometry to dimension

8. Place the dimension in between the two selected lines.

7. Pick this line as the 2nd geometry to dimension

❖ When two parallel lines are selected, the **Dimension** command will create a dimension measuring the distance in between.

9. On you own, confirm there are four dimensions applied to the sketch that appear as shown.

Modifying the dimensions of the sketch

1. Click on the **Select** icon in the *Sketcher* toolbar as shown. The **Select** command allows us to perform several modification operations on the sketched geometry and dimensions.

2. Modify the overall height-dimension.

2. Select the overall height dimension of the sketch by **double-clicking** with the left-mouse-button on the dimension text.

3. In the *Dimension Value* box, the current length of the line is displayed. Enter **3** as the new value for the dimension.

4. Press the **ENTER** key once to accept the entered value.

➤ *Pro/ENGINEER* will update the sketch using the entered dimension value. Since the other dimensions are much larger, the sketch becomes greatly distorted. We will take a different approach to modify the geometry.

5. Click on the **Undo** icon in the *Standard* toolbar to undo the **Modify Dimension** performed.

➤ Notice that the **Redo** icon is also available in the *Standard* toolbar.

6. In the pull-down menu area, click on **Edit** to display the option list and select the following option items:

Edit → **Select** → **All** (Note that Crtl+Alt+A can also activate this option.)

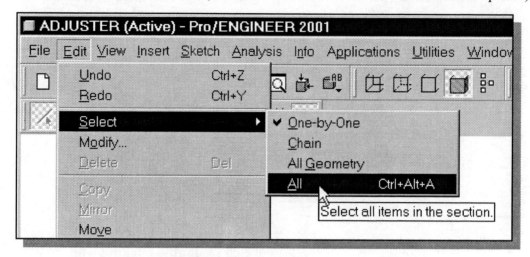

7. In the *Sketcher* toolbar, click on the **Modify** icon as shown.

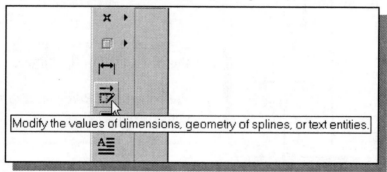

• With the pre-selection option, all dimensions are selected and listed in the *Modify Dimensions* dialog box.

8. Turn *off* the **Regenerate** option by left-clicking once on the option as shown.

9. On you own, adjust the dimensions as shown below. Note that the dimension selected in the *Modify Dimensions* dialog box is identified with an enclosed box in the display area.

10. Inside the *Modify Dimensions* dialog box, click on the **Accept** button to regenerate the sketched geometry and exit the Modify Dimensions command.

Repositioning Dimensions

1. Confirm the **Select** icon, in the *Sketcher* toolbar, is activated as shown.

2. Press and hold down the left-mouse-button on any dimension text, then drag the dimension to a new location in the display area. (Note the cursor is changed to a hand icon during this operation.)

Step 5: Completing the Base Solid Feature

❖ Now that the 2D sketch is completed, we will proceed to the next step: creating a 3D part from the 2D section. Extruding a 2D section is one of the common methods that can be used to create 3D parts. We can extrude planar faces along a path. In *Pro/ENGINEER*, each plane has a positive side and a negative side. The current sketch we're working on is set to extrude in the positive side of DTM3.

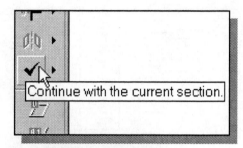

1. In the *Sketcher* toolbar, click on the **Accept** icon to end the *Pro/ENGINEER 2D Sketcher* and proceed to the next element of the feature definition.

2. In the **Spec To** submenu, confirm **Blind** is highlighted as shown.

3. Click on **Done** to proceed with the blind extrusion option.

• Note that the **Blind** option allows us to enter a value to define the depth of the extrusion.

4. In the message area, enter **2.5** as the extrusion depth.

5. In the message area, click on the **Accept** button to proceed with the feature definition.

❖ In the message area, the message "*All elements have been defined*" is displayed. We can proceed to create the solid feature.

⇨ Enter depth 2.50
⇨ Select element(s) to redefine or actions from the dialog box.

Required elements are defined

6. We are now returned to the feature dialogue box with all the required elements defined. Click on the **OK** icon to create the solid feature.

➤ Note that all dimensions disappeared from the screen. All parametric definitions are stored in the **_Pro/ENGINEER_ database** and any of the parametric definitions can be displayed and edited at any time.

The Third Dynamic Viewing Function

3D Dynamic Rotation – [Ctrl] key and [middle mouse button]

Hold down the **[Ctrl]** key and press down the middle-mouse-button in the display area. Drag the mouse on the screen to rotate the model about the screen.

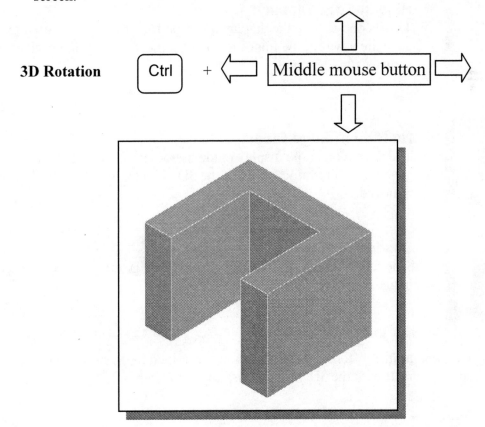

3D Rotation   Ctrl   +   ⇐   Middle mouse button   ⇒

Display Modes: Wireframe, Shaded, Hidden Edge, No Hidden

- The display in the graphics window has three display-modes: wireframe, hidden edge displayed as hidden lines, no hidden lines, and shaded image. To change the display mode in the active window, click on one of the display mode buttons on the *Standard* toolbar, as shown in the figure below.

❖ **Wireframe Image:**
The first icon in the display mode button group allows the display of 3D objects using the basic wireframe representation scheme.

❖ **Hidden-Edge Display:**
The second icon in the display mode button group can be used to generate a wireframe image of the 3D object with all the back lines shown as hidden lines.

❖ **No Hidden-Edge Display:**
The third icon in the display mode button group can be used to generate a wireframe image of the 3D object with all the back lines removed.

❖ **Shaded Solid:**
The fourth icon in the display mode button group generates a shaded image of the 3D object.

➢ On your own, use the different viewing options described in the above sections to familiarize yourself with the 3D viewing/display commands.

Step 6: Adding additional features

- Next, we will create another extrusion feature that will be added to the existing solid object.

   1. In the **Menu Manager** window, select
      Feature → Create → Solid → Protrusion

   2. In the **SOLID OPTS** submenu, select
      Extrude → Solid → Done

   3. In the **ATTRIBUTES** submenu, select
      One Side → Done

   4. Pick the right vertical face of the solid model as the sketching plane.

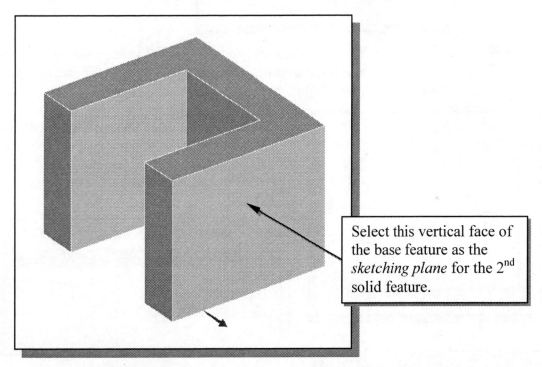

Select this vertical face of the base feature as the *sketching plane* for the 2nd solid feature.

   5. In the **DIRECTION** submenu, pick **Okay** to accept the extrusion direction as shown in the figure above.

   6. In the **SKET VIEW** submenu, pick **Top**.

7. In the display area, pick the top face of the base feature as shown.

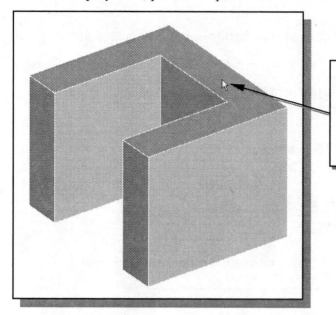

Select the top face of the base feature as the *reference plane* to set the orientation of the sketch plane.

8. Note that the top surface of the solid model and **DTM3** are pre-selected as the sketching references. In the graphics area, the two references are highlighted and displayed with two dashed lines.

9. Select the right edge and the bottom edge of the base feature so that the four sides of the selected sketching plan, or corresponding datum planes, are used as references as shown.

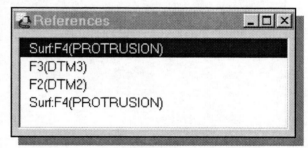

10. In the *References* dialog box, click on the **Close** button to accept the selections.

11. In the *Sketcher* toolbar, click on the **Rectangle** icon as shown to activate the **Create Rectangle** command.

12. Create a rectangle by clicking on the lower left corner of the solid model as shown below.

13. Move the cursor downward and place the opposite corner of the rectangle along the right edge of the base solid as shown below.

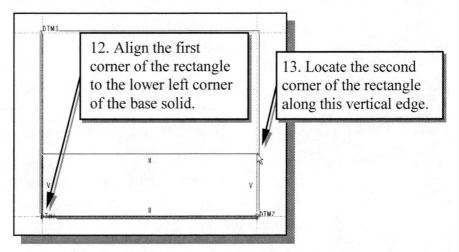

> **12. Align the first corner of the rectangle to the lower left corner of the base solid.**

> **13. Locate the second corner of the rectangle along this vertical edge.**

14. On your own, modify the height dimensions to **0.75** as shown.

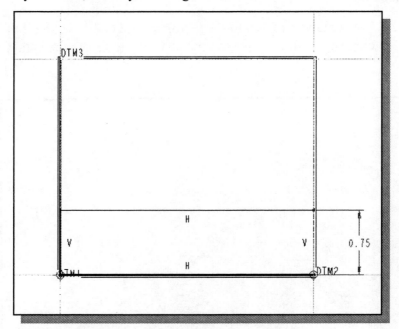

• Note that only one dimension, the height dimension, is applied to the 2D sketch; the width of the rectangle is defined by the references.

15. In the *Sketcher* toolbar, click on the **Accept** icon to end the *Pro/ENGINEER 2D Sketcher* and proceed to the next element of the feature definition.

16. In the **Spec To** submenu, confirm **Blind** is highlighted as shown.

17. Click on **Done** to proceed with the blind extrusion option.

- Note that the **Blind** option allows us to enter a value to define the depth of the extrusion.

18. In the message area, enter **2.5** as the extrusion depth.

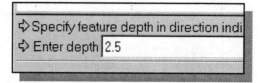

19. In the message area, click on the **Accept** button to proceed with the feature definition.

20. We are now returned to the feature dialogue box with all the required elements defined. Click on the **OK** icon to create the solid feature.

Creating a CUT Feature

- We will create a circular cut as the next solid feature of the design.

1. In the **Menu Manager** window, select

   Feature → Create → Solid → Cut

2. In the **SOLID OPTS** submenu, confirm the **Extrude** and **Solid** options are highlighted, then select **Done**.

   Extrude → Solid → Done

❖ The *CUT: Extrude* feature dialog box appears on the screen. We will need to define all elements listed to complete the feature.

3. In the **ATTRIBUTES** submenu, select

   One Side → Done

❖ Next, *Pro/ENGINEER* expects us to define and orient the sketching plane to create the 2D section required for the cut feature. Note that the procedure in creating a *cut feature* is almost the same as creating a *protrusion feature*.

Define and Orient the Sketching Plane

1. We will use the top of the cylinder as the sketching plane. Click once, with the left-mouse-button, inside the top surface of the rectangular solid feature as shown in the figure below.

2. A red arrow appears on the screen, and the message "*Arrow shows direction of feature creation. Pick FLIP or OKAY.*" is displayed in the message area. The arrow direction indicates the direction of extrusion. Make sure the arrow is pointing downward as shown in the below figure. In the **DIRECTION** submenu, pick **Okay**.

3. In the **SKET VIEW** submenu, pick **Right**.

4. Pick the right vertical face of the second solid feature as the reference plane, which will be oriented toward the right edge of the computer screen.

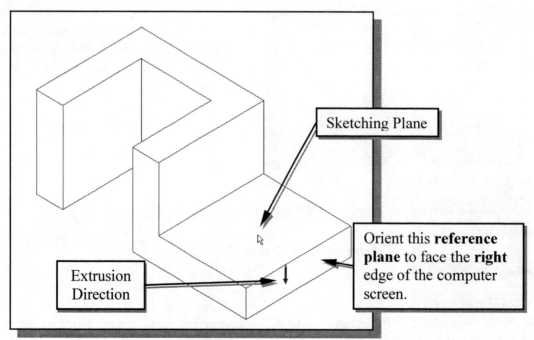

- *Pro/ENGINEER* will now align and orient the sketching plane to the computer screen. Note that the extrusion direction is aligned perpendicular to the screen.

Creating the 2D Section of the CUT Feature

1. Note that no references are pre-selected for the new sketch.

- At least one horizontal reference and one vertical reference are required to position a 2D sketch.

2. Select **the right surface of the solid model** and **DTM3** as the horizontal and sketching references as shown. In the graphics area, the two references are highlighted and displayed with two dashed lines.

3. Click on the **Close** button to accept the selected references and proceed to entering the *Pro/ENGINEER Sketcher* module.

4. In the *Sketcher* toolbar, select **Circle** as shown. The default option is to create a circle by specifying the center point and a point through which the circle will pass. The message "*Select the center of a circle*" is displayed in the message area.

5. On your own, create a circle of arbitrary size on the sketching plane as shown.

6. On your own, edit/modify the dimensions as shown.

7. Inside the *Modify Dimensions* dialog box, click on the **Accept** button to regenerate the sketched geometry and exit the Modify Dimensions command.

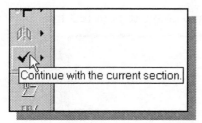

8. In the *Sketcher* toolbar, click on the **Accept** icon to exit the *Pro/ENGINEER 2D Sketcher* and proceed to the next element of the feature definition.

9. Confirm the arrow points toward the center of the circle, and pick **Okay** to continue.

10. In the **SPEC TO** submenu, select the **Thru All** option as shown.

11. Click on **Done** to proceed with the extrusion option.

• Note that the **Thru All** option does not require us to enter a value to define the depth of the extrusion; *Pro/ENGINEER* will calculate the required value to assure the extrusion is through the entire solid model.

❖ We are now returned to the feature dialogue box with all the required elements defined.

12. In the feature dialog box, click on the **OK** button to create the cut feature.

Save the Part and Exit

1. Select **Save** in the *Standard* toolbar, or you can also use the "**Ctrl-S**" combination (press down the **[Ctrl]** key and hit the **[S]** key once) to save the part.

2. In the message area, the part name is displayed. Click on the **Accept** button to save the file.

❖ It is a good habit to save your model periodically, just in case something might go wrong while you are working on it. In general, you should save your work onto the disk at an interval of every 15 to 20 minutes. You should also save before you make any major modifications to the model.

3. Use the left-mouse-button and click on **File** at the top of the *Pro/ENGINEER* main window, then choose **Exit** from the pull-down menu.

Questions:

1. What is the first thing we should set up in *Pro/ENGINEER* when creating a new model?

2. How does the *Intent Manager* assist us in sketching?

3. How do we reposition dimensions in the *Sketcher*?

4. List three of the geometric constraint symbols used by the *Pro/ENGINEER Sketcher*.

5. How many definitions are required to define a protrusion-extrude feature?

6. Describe the steps required to define the orientation of the sketching plane?

7. Identify the following commands:

   (a)

   (b)

   Ctrl + Left mouse button

   (c)

   Ctrl + Right mouse button

Exercises: (All dimensions are in inches.)

1.   Plate Thickness: 0.25

2.   Plate Thickness: 0.5

3.

4.

Notes:

Lesson 2
Constructive Solid Geometry Concepts

Learning Objectives

When you have completed this lesson, you will be able to:
- ◆ Understand the Constructive Solid Geometry Concepts.
- ◆ Create a Binary Tree.
- ◆ Understand the basic Boolean Operations.
- ◆ Set up GRID and SNAP intervals.
- ◆ Understand the importance of Order of Features.
- ◆ Create Placed Features.
- ◆ Use the different Extrusion options.

Introduction

In the 1980s, one of the main advancements in **solid modeling** was the development of the **Constructive Solid Geometry** (CSG) method. CSG describes the solid model as combinations of basic three-dimensional shapes (**primitive solids**). The basic primitive solid set typically includes: Rectangular-prism (Block), Cylinder, Cone, Sphere, and Torus (Tube). Two solid objects can be combined into one object in various ways, and these operations are known as **Boolean operations**. There are three basic Boolean operations: **JOIN (Union)**, **CUT (Difference)**, and **INTERSECT**. The JOIN operation combines the two volumes included in the different solids into a single solid. The CUT operation subtracts the volume of one solid object from the other solid object. The INTERSECT operation keeps only the volume common to both solid objects. The CSG method is also known as the **Machinist's Approach**, as the method is parallel to machine shop practices.

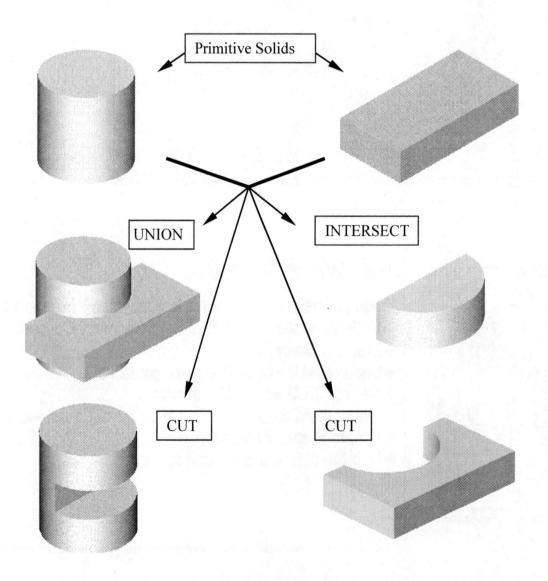

Binary Tree

Constructive Solid Geometry (CSG) is also referred to as the method used to store a solid model in the database. The resulting solid can be easily represented by what is called a **binary tree**. In a binary tree, the terminal branches (leaves) are the various primitives that are linked together to make the final solid object (the root). The binary tree is an effective way to keep track of the *history* of the resulting solid. By keeping track of the history, the solid model can be re-built by relinking through the binary tree. This provides a convenient way to modify the model. We can make modifications at the appropriate links in the binary tree and relink the rest of the history tree without building a new model.

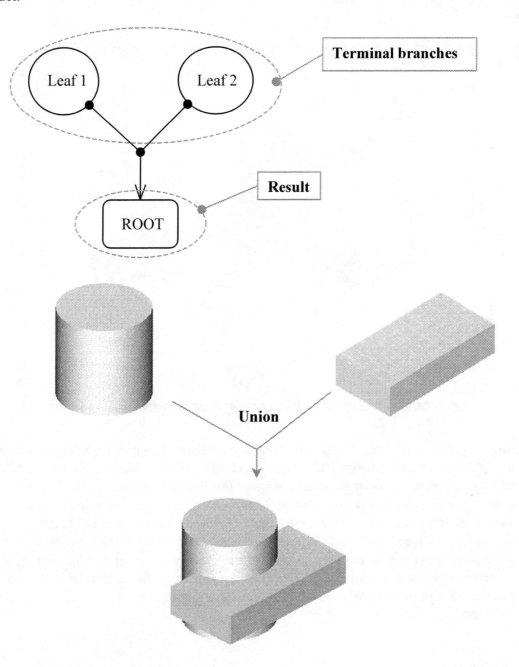

The *Locator* Design

The CSG concept is one of the important building blocks for feature-based modeling. In *Pro/ENGINEER*, the CSG concept can be used as a planning tool to determine the number of features that are needed to construct the model. It is also a good practice to create features that parallel the manufacturing process required for the design. With parametric modeling, we are no longer limited to using only the predefined basic solid shapes. In fact, any solid features we create in *Pro/ENGINEER* are used as primitive solids; parametric modeling allows us to maintain full control of the design variables that are used to describe the features. In this lesson, a more in-depth look at the parametric modeling procedure is presented. The equivalent CSG operation for each feature is also illustrated.

➢ Before going through the tutorial, on your own make a sketch of a CSG binary tree of the *Locator* design using only two basic types of primitive solids: cylinder and rectangular prism. In your sketch, how many *Boolean operations* will be required to create the model? What is your choice for the first primitive solid to use, and why? Take a few minutes to consider these questions and do the preliminary planning by sketching on a piece of paper. Compare the sketch you make to the CSG binary tree steps shown on the next page. Note that there are many different possibilities in combining the basic primitive solids to form the desired solid model. Even for the simplest design, it is possible to take several different approaches to creating the same solid model.

Modeling Strategy - CSG Binary Tree

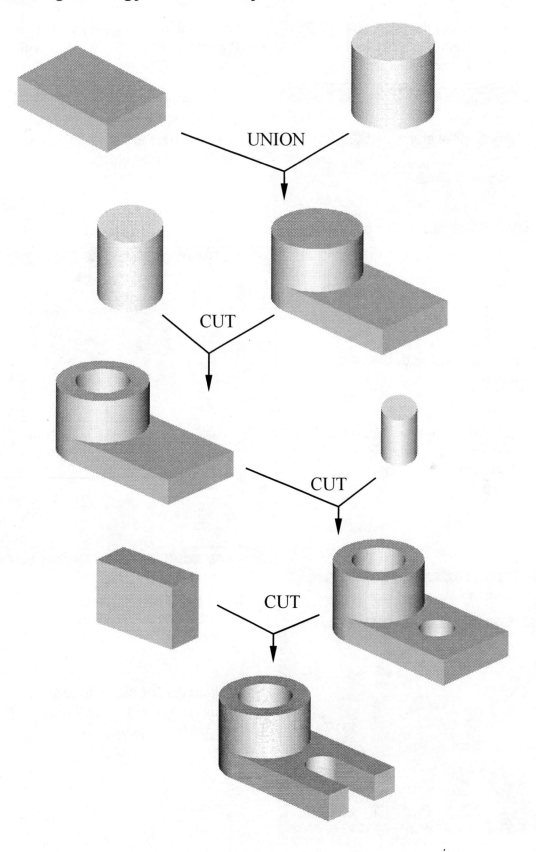

Starting *Pro/ENGINEER*

1. Select the **Pro/ENGINEER** icon on the desktop or type [***proe***] at your system prompt to start *Pro/ENGINEER*. The *Pro/ENGINEER* main window will appear on the screen.

2. Select **File** in the pull-down menus. Pick the **New** option. Notice that we can also use the key combination **Ctrl-N** to start a new object.

3. In the *New* form, enter **Locator** as the solid part file **Name**.

4. Turn *off* the **Use default template** option.

5. Pick **OK** to continue. The *Model Tree* window and the **Menu Manager** window appear on the screen.

Enter **Locator**

6. In the *New File Options* dialogue box, select **Empty** in the option list to not use any template file.

7. Click on the **OK** button to accept the settings and enter the *Pro/ENGINEER Part Modeling* mode.

Units Setup

1. Select **Set Up** in the **Menu Manager** window. In the **Menu Manager** window, the **Set Up** submenu is displayed underneath the **PART** menu.

2. Select the **Units** option. Notice that more submenu selections are displayed.

3. In the **Principal Systems of Units** form, the *Pro/ENGINEER* default setting **Inch Ibm Second** is displayed. The set of units is stored with the model file when you save. Select **millimeter Newton Second (mmNs)** from the Systems of Units.

4. Click on the **Set** button to accept the selection.

5. In the *Warning* dialog box, click on the **OK** button to accept the change of the units.

6. Click on the **Close** button to exit the *Units Manager* dialog box.

7. Pick **Done** to exit the **PART SETUP** submenu.

7. Pick *Done*

Adding the First Part Features — Datum Planes

❖ *Pro/ENGINEER* provides many powerful tools for model creation. In doing feature-based parametric modeling, it is a good practice to establish three reference planes to locate the part in space. The reference planes can be used as location references in feature constructions.

➤ Move the cursor toward the right side of the main window and click on the **Datum Plane** icon as shown.

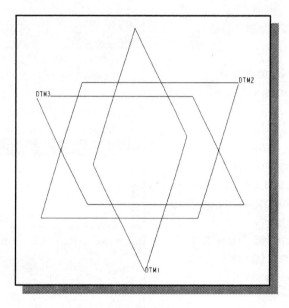

Base Feature

In *parametric modeling*, the first solid feature is called the **base feature,** which usually is the primary shape of the model. Depending upon the design intent, additional features are added to the base feature.

Some of the considerations involved in selecting the base feature:

- **Design Intent** - Determine the functionality of the design; identify the feature that is central to the design.

- **Order of features** – Choose the feature that is the logical base in terms of the order of features in the design.

- **Ease of making modifications** - Select the feature that is more stable and is less likely to be changed.

We will create a rectangular block as the base feature of the *Locator* design.

1. In the **Menu Manager** window, select

   Feature → Create → Solid → Protrusion

2. In the **SOLID OPTS** submenu, confirm the **Extrude** and **Solid** options are highlighted, then select **Done**.

   Extrude → Solid → Done

❖ The protrusion's feature dialog box appears on the screen. We will need to define all elements listed to complete the feature.

3. In the **ATTRIBUTES** submenu, select

   One Side → Done

Defining the Sketching Plane

1. We will use datum plane **DTM2** as the sketching plane. Use the left-mouse-button and click on either the edge or the nametag of the datum plane.

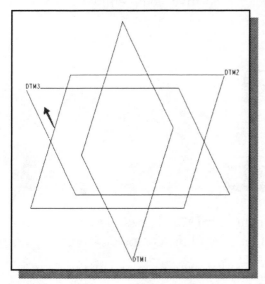

2. A red arrow appears on the edge of **DTM2**, and the message "*Arrow shows direction of feature creation. Pick Flip or Okay.*" is displayed in the message area. The arrow direction indicates the direction of the feature we are creating. In this case, it is the **direction of extrusion**. Confirm the arrow is pointing upward from **DTM2** as shown in the figure.

Defining the Orientation of the Sketching Plane

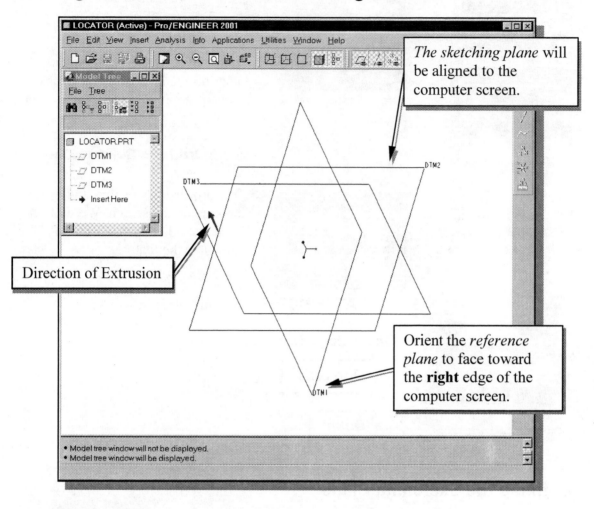

The sketching plane will be aligned to the computer screen.

Direction of Extrusion

Orient the *reference plane* to face toward the **right** edge of the computer screen.

1. In the **SKET VIEW** submenu, pick **Right**.

2. In the display area, pick the positive side (yellow side) of DTM1.

1. Pick *Right*

2. Pick *DTM1*

❖ *Pro/Engineer* will now rotate the three datum planes: DTM2 aligned to the screen and the positive side of DTM1 facing toward the right edge of the computer screen.

Creating a 2D Sketch

❖ The first thing that *Pro/ENGINEER Sketcher* expects us to do, which is displayed in the **Menu Manager** window, is to specify **sketching references**. In the previous sections, we created the three datum planes to help orient the model in 3D space; now we need to orient the 2D sketch with respect to the three datum planes. At least two references are required to orient in the horizontal direction and in the vertical direction. By default, the two planes (in our example, **DTM1** and **DTM3**) that are perpendicular to the sketching plane (**DTM2**) are automatically selected.

1. Note that **DTM1** and **DTM3** are pre-selected as the sketching references. In the graphics area, the two references are highlighted and displayed with two dashed lines. Click on **Close** to accept the selections.

2. Click on the **Model Tree** icon to toggle *off* the display of the *Model Tree*.

3. Click on the **Grid** icon to switch *on* the grid display.

4. Create a rectangle as shown, with one corner on the vertical axis (**DTM1**). (Do not be concerned if the dimensional values on your screen are different than what are shown here. We will modify the values in the following sections. Place points near the grid-points shown.)

First point near grid-point (0,3)

Second point near grid-point (7,-3)

5. Use the left mouse button and modify the dimensional values as shown. (**75mm X 50mm**)

6. In the *Sketcher* toolbar, click on the **Accept** icon to exit the *Pro/ENGINEER 2D Sketcher* and proceed to the next element of the feature definition.

7. In the **SPEC TO** submenu, confirm **Blind** is highlighted as shown.

8. Click on **Done** to proceed with the blind extrusion option.

• Note that the **Blind** option allows us to enter a value to define the depth of the extrusion.

9. In the message area, enter **15** as the extrusion depth.

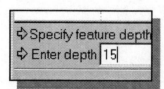

10. In the message area, click on the **Accept** button to proceed with the feature definition.

11. We are now returned to the feature dialogue box with all the required elements defined. Click on the **OK** button to create the solid feature.

➢ Note that all dimensions disappeared from the screen. All parametric definitions are stored in the *Pro/ENGINEER* **database** and any of the parametric definitions can be displayed and edited at anytime.

12. Pick the **Default Orientation** option in the pull-down menus.

Creating the Second Solid Feature

❖ We will create a cylinder as the second solid feature of the *Locator*.

1. In the **Menu Manager** window, select

Feature → Create → Solid → Protrusion

2. In the **SOLID OPTS** submenu, confirm the **Extrude** and **Solid** options are highlighted, then select **Done**.

Extrude → Solid → Done

❖ The protrusion's feature dialog box appears on the screen. We will need to define all elements listed to complete the feature.

3. In the **ATTRIBUTES** submenu, select

One Side → Done

Defining the Sketching Plane

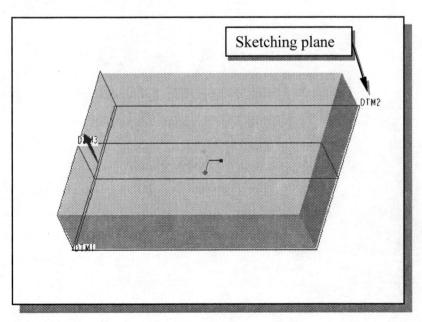

1. We will use datum plane DTM2 as the *sketching plane*. Pick **DTM2**.

2. A red arrow appears on one of the edges of DTM2, and the message "*Arrow shows direction of feature creation. Pick FLIP or OKAY.*" is displayed in the message area. The arrow direction indicates the direction of extrusion. Make sure the arrow is pointing upward from DTM2. In the **DIRECTION** submenu, pick **Okay**.

3. In the **SKET VIEW** submenu, pick **Right**.

4. In the display area, pick the right face of the base as shown.

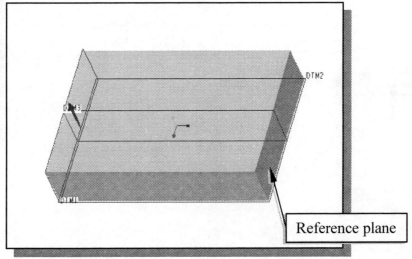

Reference plane

Creating the 2D Sketch

1. Select

1. Note that the **right surface of the solid model** and **DTM3** are pre-selected as the sketching references. In the graphics area, the two references are highlighted and displayed with two dashed lines. Click on the **Surf F4** reference in the references dialog box.

2. Click on the **Delete** button to remove the reference to the right surface of the base feature.

3. We will add two additional references. Click on **DTM1** and the **top edge** of the base feature as shown.

4. In the *References* dialog box, the two references are added to the list. Click on the **Close** button to accept the selections.

5. In the *Sketcher* toolbar, select **Circle** as shown. The default option is to create a circle by specifying the center point and a point through which the circle will pass. The message "*Select the center of a circle*" is displayed in the message area.

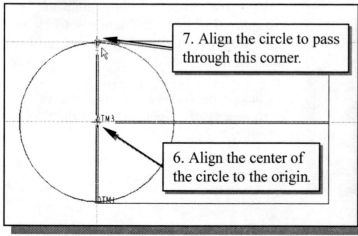

7. Align the circle to pass through this corner.

6. Align the center of the circle to the origin.

6. Move the cursor along the axes and watch for the alignment symbol. Pick the origin as the center of the circle.

7. Pick the top corner of the base feature to create the circle.

- The circle is fully defined and no dimension is needed. The selected references, which are aligned to the base solid, control the size of the circle.

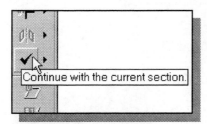

8. In the *Sketcher* toolbar, click on the **Accept** icon to exit the *Pro/ENGINEER 2D Sketcher* and proceed to the next element of the feature definition.

9. In the **SPEC TO** submenu, confirm **Blind** is highlighted as shown.

10. Click on **Done** to proceed with the blind extrusion option.

- Note that the **Blind** option allows us to enter a value to define the depth of the extrusion.

11. In the message area, enter **40** as the extrusion depth.

12. In the message area, click on the **Accept** button to proceed with the feature definition.

13. We are now returned to the feature dialogue box with all the required elements defined. Click on the **OK** icon to create the solid feature.

Creating a CUT Feature

- We will create a circular cut as the next solid feature of the **Locator**.

1. In the **Menu Manager** window, select

    Feature → Create → Solid → Cut

2. In the **SOLID OPTS** submenu, confirm the **Extrude** and **Solid** options are highlighted, then select **Done**.

    Extrude → Solid → Done

❖ The *CUT: Extrude* feature dialog box appears on the screen. We will need to define all elements listed to complete the feature.

3. In the **ATTRIBUTES** submenu, select

    One Side → Done

❖ Next, *Pro/ENGINEER* expects us to define and orient the sketching to create the 2D section required for the cut feature. Note that the procedure in creating a *cut feature* is almost the same as creating a *protrusion feature*.

Defining and Orienting the Sketching Plane

1. We will use the top of the cylinder as the sketching plane. Click once, with the left-mouse-button, inside the top surface of the cylinder.

2. A red arrow appears on the screen, and the message "*Arrow shows direction of feature creation. Pick FLIP or OKAY.*" is displayed in the message area. The arrow direction indicates the direction of extrusion. Make sure the arrow is pointing downward as shown in the figure below. In the **DIRECTION** submenu, pick **Okay**.

3. In the **SKET VIEW** submenu, pick **Right**.

4. Pick the right face of the base feature as the reference plane, and orient the face toward the right edge of the computer screen.

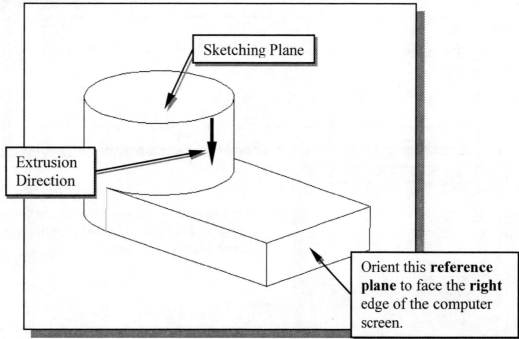

Sketching Plane

Extrusion Direction

Orient this **reference plane** to face the **right** edge of the computer screen.

❖ *Pro/ENGINEER* will now align and orient the sketching plane to the computer screen. Note that the extrusion direction is aligned perpendicular to the screen.

Creating the 2D Section of the CUT Feature

1. Note that **the right surface of the solid model** and **DTM3** are pre-selected as the sketching references. In the graphics area, the two references are highlighted and displayed with two dashed lines. Click on the **Surf F4** reference in the references dialog box.

2. Click on the **Delete** button to remove the referencing of the right surface of the base feature.

3. We will use **DTM1** as a reference in the horizontal direction. Click on **DTM1** as shown in the figure below.

4. In the *References* dialog box, the two references are listed, DTM3 and DTM1. Click on the **Close** button to accept the selections.

5. In the *Sketcher* toolbar, select **Circle** as shown. The default option is to create a circle by specifying the center point and a point through which the circle will pass. The message "*Select the center of a circle*" is displayed in the message area.

6. Move the cursor along the axes and watch for the alignment symbol. Pick the origin as the center of the circle.

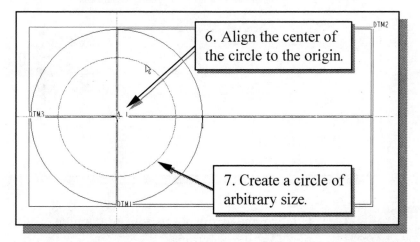

6. Align the center of the circle to the origin.

7. Create a circle of arbitrary size.

7. Pick a point inside the top surface of the cylinder and create a circle of arbitrary size.

8. On your own, modify the diameter to **40mm**.

9. Click on the **Repaint** icon to redisplay the graphics area.

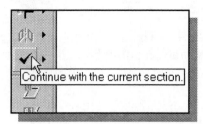

10. In the *Sketcher* toolbar, click on the **Accept** icon to exit the *Pro/ENGINEER 2D Sketcher* and proceed to the next element of the feature definition.

11. Confirm the arrow points toward the center of the circle, and pick **Okay** to continue.

12. In the **SPEC TO** submenu, select the **Thru All** option as shown.

13. Click on **Done** to proceed with the extrusion option.

• Note that the **Thru All** option does not require us to enter a depth value; instead, *Pro/ENGINEER* will calculate the depth of the extrusion to cut through the solid model.

❖ We are now returned to the feature dialogue box with all the required elements defined. Prior to creating the feature, we can preview and/or modify any of the elements that are currently defined.

14. Pick the **Default Orientation** option in the pull-down menus.

15. Click on the **Preview** button to examine the current solid feature.

16. Click on the **Repaint** icon to redisplay the graphics area.

Redefine a Feature Element

❖ Quite often during the design stage, minor modifications become necessary as the model is being formed. We will illustrate the flexibility and functionality of the feature based modeling concept by redefining one of the elements of the feature.

    1. In the feature dialogue box, select **Section**.

    2. Pick **Define** in the feature dialogue box.

    3. Pick **Sketch** in the **Menu Manager** window.

❖ We are returned to the 2D *Sketcher* and notice the **Modify** command is activated in the *Sketcher* toolbar.

    4. Pick the dimension text of the circle.

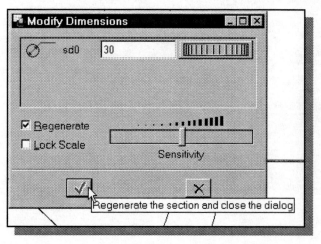

    5. In the *Modify Dimensions* dialog box, enter **30mm** as the new dimension value.

    6. Click on the **Accept** icon to adjust the geometry.

7. In the *Sketcher* toolbar, click on the **Accept** icon to end the *Pro/ENGINEER 2D Sketcher*.

8. In the feature dialogue box, pick **OK** to create the cut feature.

CSG CUT

Creating a Placed HOLE Feature

1. In the **Menu Manager** window, select

   Feature → Create → Solid → Hole

   ❖ The *Placed Hole* dialog box appears on the screen; we will set up the required elements in the different sections displayed.

2. In the **Hole Type** section, select

   Straight hole

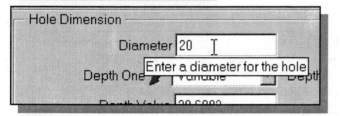

3. In the **Hole Dimension** section, enter **20** as the hole diameter.

4. In the **Hole Dimension** section, set **Depth One** to **Thru All** as shown below.

5. In the **Hole Placement** section, the **Primary Reference** is activated and *Pro/ENGINEER* expects us to select a placement reference for the center of the hole.

6. Pick the top face of the base feature as the **placement plane**.

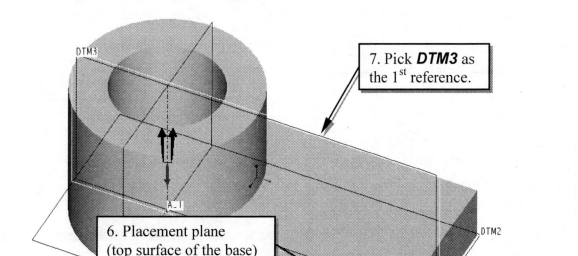

7. Pick **DTM3** as the 1st reference.

6. Placement plane (top surface of the base)

8. Pick this top edge as the 2nd reference.

❖ We then need to select two datum (edges) for the location of the hole.

7. Pick plane **DTM3** as the *first* Linear Reference.

8. Pick the top-right edge of the base as the *second* Linear Reference.

9. Enter **0** and **30** in the **Distance** boxes as shown in the figure above. (Press the **ENTER** key once as each of the values are typed in the **Distance** boxes.)

10. Click on the **Accept** icon and proceed to create the hole feature.

> ➤ The last two features we have created produce the same result even though they are accomplished by using two different approaches. The **CUT** command is more flexible in the shape that can be used, but it also requires the definition of more elements.

Creating the Final Feature

❖ We will create a rectangular cut as the final solid feature of the **Locator**.

1. In the **Menu Manager** window, select

   Feature → Create → Solid → Cut

2. In the **SOLID OPTS** submenu, confirm the **Extrude** and **Solid** options are highlighted then select **Done**.

3. In the **ATTRIBUTES** submenu, select **One Side → Done**

Defining and Orienting the Sketching Plane

❖ On your own, select the **right face** of the base feature as the sketching plane. Pick the
top face of the base feature as the reference plane, and orient the face toward the top
edge of the computer screen.

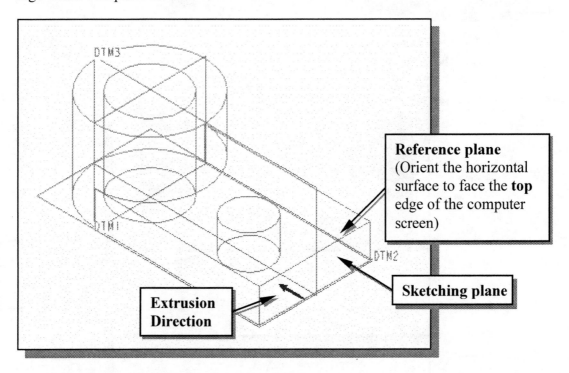

> **Reference plane**
> (Orient the horizontal
> surface to face the **top**
> edge of the computer
> screen)

Sketching plane

**Extrusion
Direction**

Creating the 2D Section

1. Use **DTM2, DTM3,** and the top surface of the base feature as the references
for the 2D sketch. *Pro/ENGINEER* will use these references to assure the 2D
sketch is created at the right location.

> Pick these edges as
> References

2. In the *Sketcher* toolbar, click on the **Rectangle** icon as shown to activate the Rectangle command.

3. Create a rectangle as shown, with one corner on the horizontal axis (DTM2) and the other on the top surface of the base feature.

5. Align the two corners to the references.

4. On your own, use the **Modify** command and adjust the rectangle to be **20mm** wide and centered as shown.

5. In the *Sketcher* toolbar, click on the **Accept** button to end the *Pro/ENGINEER 2D Sketcher*.

6. Confirm the direction of the material side to be removed. The arrow points toward the center of the rectangle just created. Pick **Okay** to continue.

7. Confirm the direction of the cut. (Use the *Dynamic Viewing* functions to reorient the 3D view.)

8. Pick **UpTo Surface** in the option menu.

9. Pick **Done** to continue.

10. Pick the inside surface of the small hole feature.

11. Pick **OK** in the feature dialogue box to create the cut.

Questions:

1. What are the three basic *Boolean operations* commonly used in computer geometric modeling software?

2. What is a *primitive solid*?

3. What does *CSG* stand for?

4. Which Boolean operation keeps only the volume common to the two solid objects?

5. What are the differences in creating a CUT feature and creating a HOLE feature in *Pro/ENGINEER*?

6. Using the CSG concept, create Binary Tree sketches showing the steps you plan to use to create the two models shown on the next page:

Ex.1)

Ex.2)

Exercises: (All dimensions are in inches.)

1.

2.

3.

Notes:

Lesson 3
Model History Tree

Learning Objectives

When you have completed this lesson, you will be able to:
- ♦ Understand Feature Interactions.
- ♦ Use the Part Browser.
- ♦ Modify and Update Feature Dimensions
- ♦ Perform History-Based Part Modifications.
- ♦ Change the Names of created Features.
- ♦ Perform Basic Design Changes.

Introduction

In *Pro/ENGINEER*, the *design intents* are stored as features in the **history tree**. The structure of the model history tree resembles that of a **CSG binary tree**. A CSG binary tree contains only Boolean relations, while the *Pro/ENGINEER* **history tree** contains all features, including Boolean relations. A history tree is a sequential record of the features used to create the part. This history tree contains the construction steps, plus the rules defining the design intent at each construction operation. In a history tree, each time a new modeling event is created, previously defined features can be used to define information such as size, location and orientation. It is therefore important to think about your modeling strategy before you start creating anything. It is important, but also difficult, to plan ahead for all possible design changes that might occur. This approach in modeling is a major difference of **feature based cad software**, such as *Pro/ENGINEER*, from previous generation CAD systems.

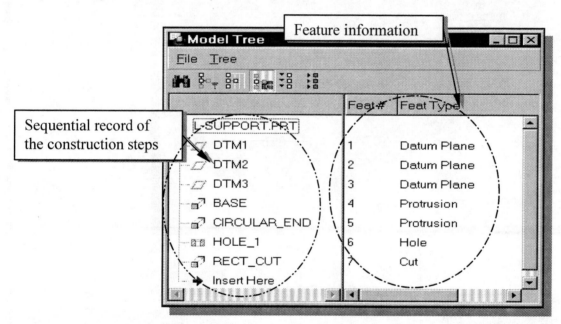

Feature-based parametric modeling is a cumulative process. Every time a new feature is added, a new result is created and the feature is also added to the history tree. The database also includes parameters of features that were used to define them. All of this happens automatically as features are created and manipulated. At this point, it is important to understand that all of this information is retained, and modifications are done based on the same input information.

In *Pro/ENGINEER*, the model tree gives information about modeling order and other information about the feature. Part modifications can be done through accessing the features in the history tree. It is important to understand the concept of the history tree when you modify parts. *Pro/ENGINEER* remembers the history of a part, including all the rules that were used to create it, so that changes can be made to any operation that was performed to create the part. To modify a feature in *Pro/ENGINEER*, you may select the feature by picking it in the display area or selecting the name of the feature in the **Model Tree** window.

The *L-Support* Design

❖ Based on your knowledge of *Pro/ENGINEER* so far, how many features would you use to create the design? Which feature would you choose as the **base feature**, the first feature, of the model? What is your choice in arranging the order of the features? Would you organize the features differently if additional fillets were to be added in the design? Take a few minutes to consider these questions and do preliminary planning by sketching on a piece of paper. You are also encouraged to create the model on your own prior to following through the tutorial.

Starting Pro/ENGINEER

1. Select the **Pro/ENGINEER** option on the *Start* menu or select the **Pro/ENGINEER** icon on the desktop to start *Pro/ENGINEER*. The *Pro/ENGINEER* main window will appear on the screen.

2. Click on the **New** icon, located in the standard toolbar as shown.

3. In the *New* dialogue box, confirm the model **Type** is set to **Part** (**Solid** Sub-type).

4. Enter **L-Support** as the part **Name** as shown in the figure.

5. Turn *off* the **Use default template** option.

6. Click on the **OK** button to accept the settings.

7. In the *New File Options* dialogue box, select **Empty** in the option list to not use any template file.

8. Click on the **OK** button to accept the settings and enter the *Pro/ENGINEER Part Modeling* mode.

Model name

❖ The *Model Tree* window and the **Menu Manager** window appeared on the screen. Notice in the *Model Tree* window, the part name is displayed. The *Pro/ENGINEER Model Tree* window presents the model structure, feature by feature, in the order in which the features are created.

• Note that clicking on the **Model Tree** icon allows us to toggle *on/off* the display of the *Model Tree* window.

9. On your own, set up the **Units** to **Inch-Pound-Second (IPS)**.

10. On your own, click on the **Datum Plane** icon and create the basic set of datum planes.

❖ In the *Model Tree* window, the datum planes are new features added into the model structure.

11. Click on **DTM1** in the *Model Tree* window and notice the selected feature is highlighted in the display area.

12. Click on **DTM2**; the selected feature is highlighted in the display area.

❖ Any selection of features can also be done through the *Model Tree* window.

Modeling Strategy

Creating the Base Feature

1. In the **Menu Manager** window, select

Feature → Create → Solid → Protrusion

2. In the **SOLID OPTS** submenu, confirm the **Extrude** and **Solid** options are highlighted, and then select **Done**.

Extrude → Solid → Done

❖ The protrusion's feature dialog box appears on the screen. We will need to define all elements listed to complete the feature.

3. In the **ATTRIBUTES** submenu, select

Both Sides → Done

Defining the Sketching Plane

1. We will use datum plane **DTM3** as the *sketch plane*. Use the left mouse button and select **DTM3** in the *Model Tree* window.

❖ As more features are created, selecting through the *Model Tree* is an extremely convenient option. As can be seen, *Pro/ENGINEER* provides us a variety of tools to aid the selection and creation of the desired features.

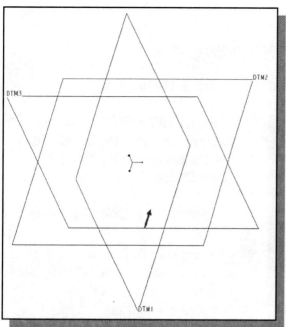

2. A red arrow appears on the edge of DTM3, and the message "*Arrow shows direction of viewing the sketching plane.*" is displayed in the message area. The arrow direction indicates the direction we will be viewing the sketching plane. Confirm the arrow is pointing upward from DTM3 as shown in the figure; pick **Okay** in the **Menu Manager** window.

3. In the **SKET VIEW** submenu, pick **Right**.

3. Pick *Right*

4. In the *Model Tree* window, pick **DTM1**.

4. Pick *DTM1*

2D Sketching

1. In the *References* dialog box, confirm **DTM1** and **DTM2** are selected as the references for the 2D sketch. Click on the **Close** button to accept the settings.

2. Create the 2D section as shown. (The lower-left corner aligned to the origin.)

3. Now that the 2D sketch is completed, we will proceed to the next *element*. In the *Sketcher* toolbar, click on the **Accept** button to end the *Pro/ENGINEER* **Sketcher** command.

Extrusion

1. In the **SPEC TO** submenu, confirm **Blind** is highlighted as shown.

2. Click on **Done** to proceed with the blind extrusion option.

- Note that the **Blind** option allows us to enter a value to define the depth of the extrusion.

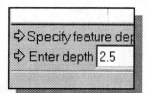

3. In the message area, enter **2.5** as the extrusion depth.

4. Pick **OK** in the feature dialog box to create the solid.

On your own, use the *Dynamic Viewing* function ([**Ctrl**] + [middle-mouse-button]) to view the 3D model. Notice the protrusion feature is added to the *Model Tree*, and **DTM3** is at the center of the extrusion.

Set up the *Pro/ENGINEER* Default View

1. Select **Utilities** in the pull-down menus. Pick the **Environment** option. The environment option allows us to adjust various display settings.

2. At the bottom of the *Environment* form, three groups of display settings are available. Pick **Isometric** as the *default view orientation*.

3. Toggle *off* the **Ring Message Bell** option to switch off the bell.

4. Pick **OK** to exit the form.

5. Use the quick key combination **Ctrl-D** to change the view orientation in the display area.

Add the Second Solid Feature

1. In the **Menu Manager** window, select

    Feature → Create → Solid → Protrusion

2. In the **SOLID OPTS** submenu, confirm the **Extrude** and **Solid** options are highlighted, and then select **Done**.

    Extrude → Solid → Done

❖ The protrusion's feature dialog box appears on the screen. We will need to define all elements listed to complete the feature.

3. In the **ATTRIBUTES** submenu, select

    One Side → Done

4. In the *Model Tree* window, pick **DTM2** as the sketching plane as shown.

5. Confirm the extrusion direction points upward as shown and click **Okay**.

6. In the **SKET VIEW** submenu, pick **Right**.

7. Select the right surface of the base feature as the orienting reference.

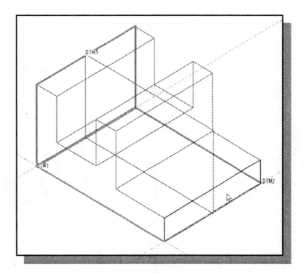

8. Click inside the display area to set the display area as the active window.

9. Use the key combination **Ctrl-D** to change the view orientation in the display area.

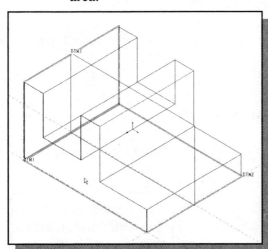

10. Select the front vertical surface of the base feature as an additional sketching reference.

11. In the *References* dialog box, three references are listed as shown. Click on the **Close** button to accept the selections.

12. In the *Sketcher* toolbar, select **Circle** as shown. The default option is to create a circle by specifying the center point and a point through which the circle will pass. The message "*Select the center of a circle*" is displayed in the message area.

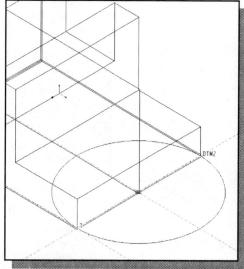

13. Align the center of the circle to the intersection of the two sketching references and create the circle as shown. (Note the **Tangent** constraint symbol)

• The circle is fully defined and no dimension is needed. The base solid controls the size of the circle.

14. Now that the 2D sketch is completed, we will proceed to the next *element*. In the **Sketcher** toolbar, click on the **Accept** button to end the *Pro/ENGINEER* Sketcher command.

❖ Note that the default extrusion direction points upward as shown.

15. Pick **Up To Curve** in the depth menu.

16. Pick **Done** in the **Menu Manager**.

17. Pick the top-edge of the horizontal surface of the base to define the extrusion distance as shown.

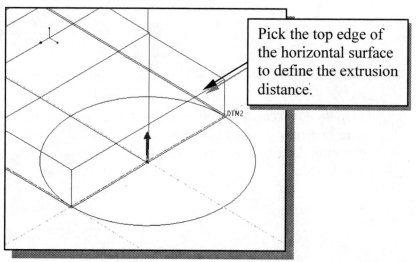

Pick the top edge of the horizontal surface to define the extrusion distance.

18. Pick **OK** in the feature dialog box to complete the feature.

19. Pick **Done** in the **Menu Manager**.

Renaming the Part Features

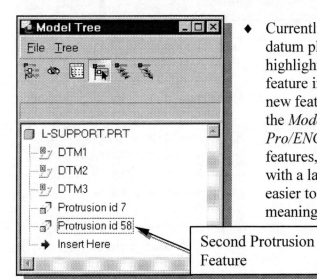

Second Protrusion Feature

♦ Currently, our model contains five features: three datum planes and two protrusions. The feature is highlighted in the display area when we select the feature in the *Model Tree* window. Each time a new feature is created, the feature is also added in the *Model Tree* window. By default, *Pro/ENGINEER* will use generic names for part features, but when we begin to deal with parts with a large number of features, it will be much easier to identify the features using more meaningful names.

1. In the **Menu Manager** window, select

   Set Up → Name

2. Confirm the selection option is set to **Feature** as shown.

3. If the *Model Tree* window disappeared, use the **Model Tree** icon to redisplay the *Model Tree* window.

4. In the *Model Tree* window, pick the first **protrusion** we created.

5. In the message area, enter **BASE** as the new feature name.

6. Inside the display area, click on the circular portion of the second protrusion feature to select the feature.

7. In the message area, enter **Circular_End** as the new feature name. (Note that *Pro/ENGINEER* does not allow spaces to be used as part of the names.)

•   In the *Model Tree* window, the new feature names are displayed as shown.

8. Pick **Done** in the **PART SETUP** menu to exit the **NAME SETUP** menu.

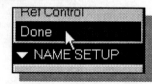

Expanding the Model Tree Listing

1. In the *Model Tree* window, click on the third icon to set the **Column display options**.

2. In the *Model Tree Columns* form, select

   [Feat #] → **[>>]**

3. In the *Model Tree Columns* form, select

   [Feat Type] → **[>>]**

4. In the **Displayed** section, set the column **Width** of **Feat #** to **3** and **Feat Type** to **14** as shown in the figure.

5. Click on the **OK** button to apply the settings and exit the form.

6. Resize the *Model Tree* window by dragging the edge of the window with the left-mouse-button to look at the different feature information.

7. On your own, examine the different icons/commands available in the *Model Tree* window.

Creating a Placed HOLE Feature

1. In the **Menu Manager** window, select

    Feature → Create → Solid → Hole

❖ The *Placed Hole* dialog box appeared on the screen; we will set up the required elements in the different sections displayed.

2. In the **Hole Type** section options, set the type to: **Straight hole**

3. In the **Hole Dimension** section, enter **1.0** as the hole **Diameter**. Set the **Depth One** option to **None** and the **Depth Two** option to **Thru All** as shown in the below figure. (Note the corresponding direction symbols shown in the display area.)

4. In the **Hole Placement** section, select the *axis* of the **Circular_End** feature (**A_1**) and note the **Placement Type** is switched to **Coaxial** automatically.

5. Select **DTM2** in the *Model Tree* window as the *placement plane* for the hole feature. (Refer to the figure on the next page for the selections.)

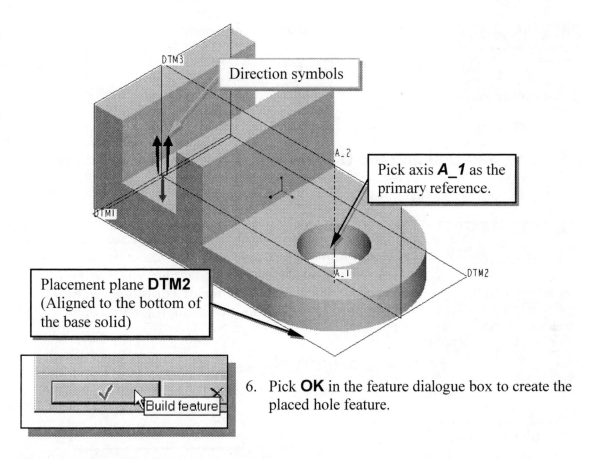

Direction symbols

Pick axis **A_1** as the primary reference.

Placement plane **DTM2** (Aligned to the bottom of the base solid)

6. Pick **OK** in the feature dialogue box to create the placed hole feature.

Creating a Rectangular Cutout

- We will create a rectangular cutout as the final solid feature of the locator.

1. In the **Menu Manager** window, select

   Feature → Create → Solid → Cut

2. In the **SOLID OPTS** submenu, confirm the **Extrude** and **Solid** options are highlighted, and then select **Done**.

   Extrude → Solid → Done

3. In the **ATTRIBUTES** submenu, select

    One Side → Done

Selecting and Defining the Orientation of the Sketching Plane

1. In the *Model Tree* window, select **DTM1** as the sketching plane

2. A red arrow appears on the screen, and the message *"Arrow shows direction of feature creation. Pick FLIP or OKAY."* is displayed in the message area. The arrow direction indicates the direction of extrusion. Pick **Flip** to change the extrusion direction as shown in the below figure.

3. In the **DIRECTION** submenu, pick **Okay**.

5. Pick the top surface to orient the sketching plane. (Top option)

2. Extrusion Direction

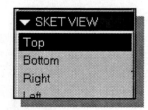

4. In the **SKET VIEW** dialog box, pick **Top**.

5. Select the top surface of the base model to orient the sketching plane. The selected plane will face toward the top edge of the computer screen.

6. In the *References* dialog box, **DTM3** and the **top horizontal plane** are selected as the *sketching references*. Click on the **Close** button to accept the settings.

7. Create a rectangle of arbitrary size, with the top edge aligned to the top surface of the solid model, as shown in the below figure.

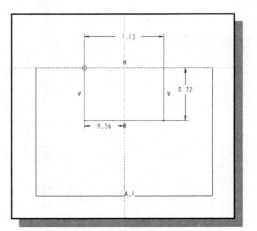

8. In the *Sketcher* toolbar, click on the **Modify** icon as shown.

9. Click on the width dimension and enter **1.5** as the new value, as shown.

10. Click on the height dimension and notice that the dimension value appears in the *Modify Dimensions* box as shown. Enter **0.75** as the new height dimension.

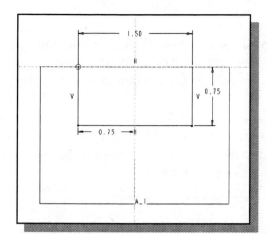

11. On your own, adjust the other dimension so that the rectangle is centered.

12. Now that the 2D sketch is completed, we will proceed to the next *element.* In the *Sketcher* toolbar, click on the **Accept** button to end the *Pro/ENGINEER* Sketcher command.

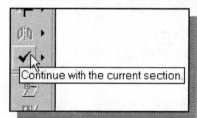

13. For the area to be removed, confirm the arrow points toward the center of the rectangle. Pick **Okay** to continue.

14. In the **Menu Manager** window, select

   Thru Next → Done

15. Pick **OK** in the feature dialog box to create the feature.

Examining the Model History

1. In the *Model Tree* window, pick **DTM1** and notice the feature is highlighted in the display area when we select the feature in the *Model Tree* window.

2. On your own, change the names of the last two features to **Hole_1** and **Rect_CUT.** Exit from any submenu and return to the **PART** menu window before continuing.

3. Pick **Hole_1** and observe the highlighted feature in the display area.

4. Select **Utilities** in the pull-down menus.

5. Pick the **Model Player** option.

6. Click on the **Go to the beginning of the model** button in the *Model Player* window as shown.

7. Click on the **Step Forward** button to look at the first feature created.

♦ Notice that we have literally gone back in time. We are at the first feature of the model.

8. On your own, click the **Step Forward** button and view the features used to create the model.

9. Click **Finish** to exit the *Model Player*.

❖ Note that the *Model Player* simply redisplays the features recorded in the *Model Tree*. The *Pro/ENGINEER Model Tree* is a sequential record of the features used to create the part. We can view and make modifications to assure the accuracy of our model at any time.

History-based Part Modifications

❖ *Pro/ENGINEER* uses the *history-based part modification* approach, which enables us to make modifications to the appropriate features in the *Model History Tree* and re-link the rest of the *History Tree*. We can think of it as going back in time and modifying some aspects of the modeling steps used to create the part. We can modify any feature that we have created. As an example, we will adjust the depth of the rectangular cutout.

1. In the *Model Tree* window, move the cursor on top of **Rect_CUT**, then press and hold down the right-mouse-button. A pop-up menu is displayed.

2. Select **Redefine**. Notice the feature dialog box appears on the screen.

3. Pick **Depth** in the **Element** window.

4. Click on the **Define** button to change the selected feature element.

5. In the **SPEC TO** menu window, select

   THRU ALL → **Done**

6. Pick **OK** in the feature dialogue box to complete the modification.

❖ As can been seen, the Pro/ENGINEER history-based modification approach is very straightforward and it only took a few seconds to do this modification.

Modifying Dimensional Values

❖ Once a feature has been created, it is very easy to modify its dimensional values in *Pro/ENGINEER*.

1. In the **PART** menu window, select

   Modify → Value

2. In the *Model Tree* window, pick the **BASE** feature as shown.

3. In the display area, the dimensions associated with the base feature are displayed. Pick the **2.0** text (width of the upper section of the part).

4. Enter **2.5** in the message area.

Modify this dimension

5. Pick **Done** in the **Modify** menu window.

6. Pick **Regenerate** in the **PART** menu window to apply the modification.

- Note that the **Modify** command can also be accessed through the use of right-mouse-button on the feature in the *Model Tree* window.

Modifying the 2D Section of the Base Feature

❖ We can also make changes to the original 2D sections we have created.

1. In the *Model Tree* window, move the cursor on top of **BASE,** then press and hold down the right-mouse-button. A pop-up menu is displayed.

2. Pick **Redefine** in the pop-up menu.

3. In the feature dialogue box, select **Section** in the feature **Element** list as shown.

4. Click on the **Define** button to change the selected element.

5. In the **SECTION** menu, pick **Sketch.**

❖ The *Pro/ENGINEER Sketcher* toolbar appears on the screen and the original 2D section is displayed in the display area. We have literally gone back in time to the point where we first created the 2D section.

6. In the *Sketcher* toolbar, select

    Sketch → Arc → Fillet

7. Pick the two lines as shown to create a fillet.

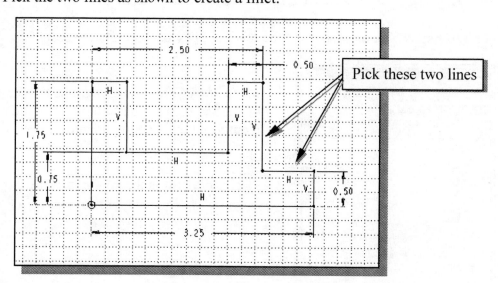

Pick these two lines

8. On your own, modify the radius of the fillet to **0.25** inches.

9. In the *Sketcher* toolbar, click on the **Accept** button to end the *Pro/ENGINEER* Sketcher command.

10. Pick **OK** in the feature dialogue box to complete the modification.

❖   In a typical design process, the initial design will undergo many analyses, testing and reviews. The *history-based part modification* approach is an extremely powerful tool that enables us to quickly update the design. At the same time, it is quite clear that PLANNING AHEAD becomes more important in doing feature-based modeling.

Questions:

1. What are stored in the *Pro/ENGINEER History Tree*?

2. When extruding, what is the difference between *Blind* and *Thru All*?

3. What is the *history-based part modification* approach?

4. What determines how a model reacts when other features in the model change?

5. Describe two methods in *Pro/ENGINEER* to access the **Modify Dimension Value** command.

6. Create *History Tree* sketches showing the steps you plan to use to create the two models shown on the next page:

Ex.1)

Ex.2)

Exercises: (All dimensions are in inches.)

1.

2.

3.

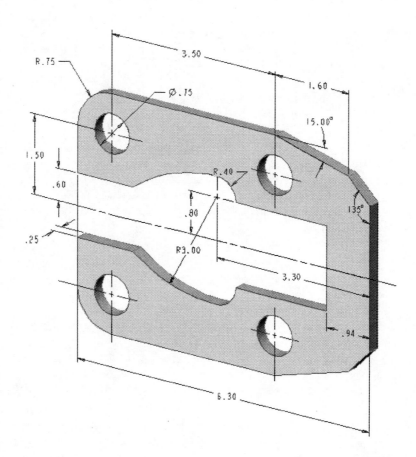

Notes:

Lesson 4
Parent/Child Relationships

Learning Objectives

When you have completed this lesson, you will be able to:
♦ Understand the Parent/Child relations between Features.
♦ Create Swept Features.
♦ Set up Multiple Work planes.
♦ Create Lofted Features
♦ Use the Shell Command.
♦ Create 3D Rounds & Fillets

Introduction

The parent/child relationship is one of the most powerful aspects of ***parametric modeling***. In *Pro/ENGINEER*, each time a new modeling event is created, previously defined features can be used to define information such as size, location, and orientation. The referenced features become **PARENT** features to the new feature, and the new feature is called the **CHILD** feature. The parent/child relationships determine how a model reacts when other features in the model change, thus capturing design intent. It is crucial to keep track of these parent/child relations. Any modification to a parent feature can change one or more of its children. As one might expect, parent/child relationships can become quite complicated when the features begin to accumulate. It is therefore important to think about the modeling strategy before we start to create anything. The main consideration is to try to plan ahead for all possible design changes that might occur which would be affected by the existing parent/child relationships.

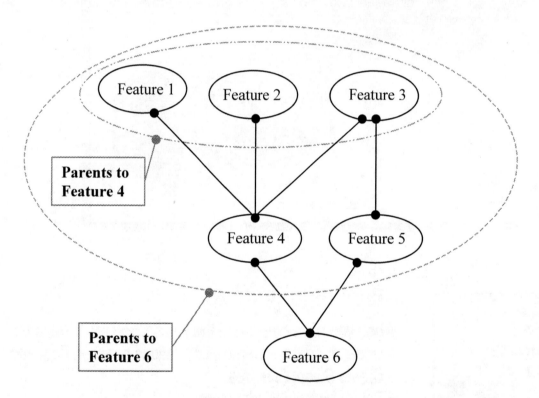

Parent/child relationships can be created *implicitly* or *explicitly*; implicit relationships are implied by the feature creation method and explicit relationships are entered manually by the user. We have been using implicit parent/child relationships in the previous lessons. For example, before creating a 2D section in the *Pro/ENGINEER Sketcher* mode, we select a sketching plane and a reference plane. Both of these become parents of the new feature. If the sketching plane is moved, the child feature will move with it. The reference plane determines the orientation of the section on the sketching plane. If the orientation is changed, the orientation of the child feature is changed as well. The use of *explicit parent/child relationships* will be demonstrated in the following lessons.

The *U-Bracket* Design

Preliminary Modeling Considerations

Prior to creating the model, a few minutes of planning and sketching on paper will save many hours of redefining the design on the computer. Two of the main modeling considerations are:

- **Design Intent** – Determine the functionality of the design; identify features that are central to the design.

- **Order of Features** – Consider the parent/child relationships necessary for all features.

➢ Based on your knowledge of *Pro/ENGINEER* so far, how many features would you use to create the model? Which feature would you choose as the **base feature**? What is your choice for arranging the order of the features? Would you organize the features differently if the rectangular cut at the center is changed to a circular shape (Radius: 80mm)? Take a few minutes to consider these questions and do preliminary planning by sketching on a piece of paper.

Starting *Pro/ENGINEER*

1. Select the **Pro/ENGINEER** icon at the desktop or type [***proe***] at your system prompt to start *Pro/ENGINEER*. The *Pro/ENGINEER* main window will appear on the screen.

2. Select **File** in the pull-down menus. Pick the **New** option. Notice that we can also use the key combination **Ctrl-N** to start a new object.

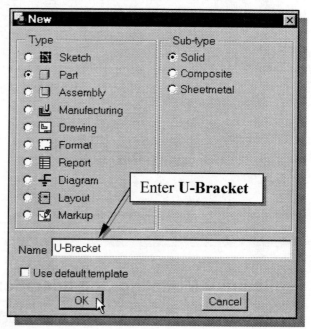

3. In the *New* form, enter ***U-Bracket*** as the solid part file **Name**.

4. Turn *off* the **Use default template** option.

5. Pick **OK** to continue. The *Model Tree* window and the **Menu Manager** window appear on the screen.

6. In the *New File Options* dialogue box, select **Empty** in the option list to not use any template file.

7. Click on the **OK** button to accept the settings and enter the *Pro/ENGINEER Part Modeling* mode.

Units Setup

1. Select **Set Up** in the **Menu Manager** window. In the Menu Manager window, the **Set Up** submenu is displayed underneath the **PART** menu.

2. Select the **Units** option. Notice that more submenu selections are displayed. .

3. In the **Systems of Units** form, the *Pro/ENGINEER* default setting **Inch Ibm Second** is displayed. The set of units is stored with the model file when you save. Select **millimeter Newton Second (mmNs***)* from the **Systems of Units**.

4. Click on the **Set** button to accept the selection.

5. In the *Warning* dialog box, click on the **OK** button to accept the change of the units.

6. Click on the **Close** button to exit the *Units Manager* dialog box.

7. Pick **Done** to exit the **PART SETUP** submenu.

7. Pick *Done*

Adding the First Part Features — Datum Planes

❖ *Pro/ENGINEER* provides many powerful tools for model creation. In doing feature-based parametric modeling, the approach to establish three reference-planes to locate the part in space is known as the Base Orphan Node technique. The reference planes can be used as location references in feature construction.

➢ Move the cursor toward the right side of the main window and click on the **Datum Plane** icon as shown. A set of three mutually perpendicular datum planes are created as the first features.

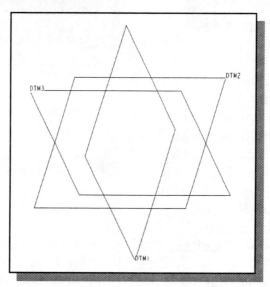

Creating the Base Feature

❖ We will create the model using four features and the base feature will be the bottom section of the model. Keep in mind that this selection is not necessarily the best selection and other choices are also feasible.

1. In the **Menu Manager** window, select

Feature → Create → Solid → Protrusion

2. In the **SOLID OPTS** submenu, confirm the **Extrude** and **Solid** options are highlighted, and then select **Done**.

Extrude → Solid → Done

❖ The protrusion's feature dialog box appears on the screen. We will need to define all elements listed to complete the feature.

3. In the **ATTRIBUTES** submenu, select

One Side → Done

Defining the Sketching Plane

1. We will use datum plane **DTM2** as the sketching plane. Use the left mouse button and click on either the edge or the nametag of the datum plane.

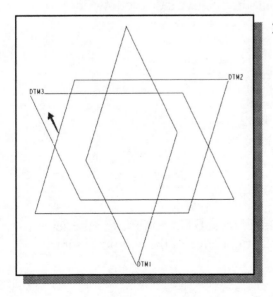

2. A red arrow appears on the edge of **DTM2**, and the message "*Arrow shows direction of feature creation. Pick Flip or Okay.*" is displayed in the message area. The arrow direction indicates the direction of the feature we are creating. In this case, it is the **direction of extrusion**. Confirm the arrow is pointing upward from **DTM2** as shown in the figure.

Define the Orientation of the Sketching Plane

1. In the **SKET VIEW** submenu, pick **Right**.

2. In the display area, pick the positive side (yellow side) of DTM1.

1. Pick *Right*

❖ *Pro/ENGINEER* will now rotate the three datum planes: DTM2 aligned to the screen and the positive side of DTM1 facing toward the right edge of the computer screen.

Creating a 2D Sketch

❖ The first thing that *Pro/ENGINEER Sketcher* expects us to do, which is displayed in the **Menu Manager** window, is to specify **sketching references**. In the previous sections, we created the three datum planes to help orient the model in 3D space; now we need to orient the 2D sketch with respect to the three datum planes. At least two references are required to orient in the horizontal direction and in the vertical direction. By default, the two planes (in our example, **DTM1** and **DTM3**) that are perpendicular to the sketching plane (**DTM2**) are automatically selected.

1. Note that **DTM1** and **DTM3** are pre-selected as the sketching references. In the graphics area, the two references are highlighted and displayed with two dashed lines. Click on **Close** to accept the selections.

2. Create a rectangle as shown, with one corner on the vertical axis (**DTM1**). (Do not be concerned if the dimensional values on your screen are different than what are shown here. We will modify the values in the following sections. Place points near the grid-points shown.)

3. In the *Sketcher* toolbar, select **Rectangle**. The message "*Pick two points to indicate diagonal of box. Use middle button to abort*" is displayed in the message area.

4. Create a rectangle, of arbitrary size, with the center of the rectangle is near the intersection of the datum planes as shown.

5. In the *Sketcher* toolbar, click on the **Arrow** icon.

6. Inside the graphics area, press down the **SHIFT** key and pick the two vertical lines with the **left-mouse-button**.

7. Inside the graphics area, press down the **right-mouse-button** and select **Delete**. *Pro/ENGINEER* will delete the two selected entities.

8. In the *Sketcher* toolbar, select **Arc**. Notice the default arc option is the **3-Points/Tangent End** option. We will select two entities and *Pro/ENGINEER* will automatically create an arc tangent to the two entities.

9. Pick the two right ends of the two horizontal lines to create an arc that is tangent to the two lines.

10. Repeat the last step and create an arc on the left side. Note the *Tangent* symbol displayed as the arcs are created.

11. In the *Sketcher* toolbar, select the **Concentric Circle** option and create two circles that are of the same size and concentric to the two arcs. (Use the **middle-mouse-button** to end the command or select a different center point.)

12. **Create** and **modify** the dimensions as shown below.

13. Now that the 2D sketch is completed, we will proceed to the next *element*. In the *Sketcher* toolbar, click on the **Accept** button to end the *Pro/ENGINEER* Sketcher command.

Blind Extrusion

1. In the **SPEC TO** submenu, pick **Done** in the Menu Manager window to proceed.

2. In the message area, enter **30** (mm) as the depth of extrusion.

3. Pick **OK** in the feature dialogue box to create the solid.

Examining the Parent/Child Relationships

The *Model Tree* shows four features: three datum planes and the base feature (the **Protrusion id 7** shown in the figure below) we just created. The parent/child relationships were established implicitly when we created the base feature: (1) datum plane DTM2 was selected as the sketch plane; (2) DTM1 was selected as the reference plane to orient the sketching plane; (3) in the *Sketcher* mode, DTM1 and DTM3 were selected as references planes.

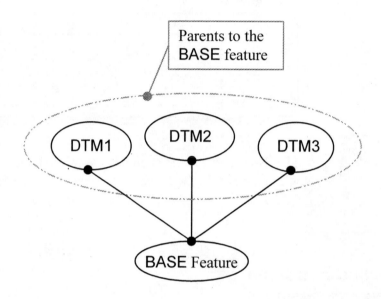

Creating the Second Solid Feature

- We will use the **Protrusion** option to create the next solid feature.

1. In the **Menu Manager** window, select

   **Feature → Create →
   Solid →
   Protrusion**

2. In the **SOLID OPTS** submenu, confirm the **Extrude** and **Solid** options are highlighted, and then select **Done**.

3. In the **ATTRIBUTES** submenu, select

   Both Sides → Done

4. Pick datum plane **DTM3** as the *sketching plane* (an arrow points toward the back face of the solid) and **DTM2** as the *reference plane* facing toward the **top** edge of the computer screen.

5. Accept the use of DTM1 and DTM2 as the sketching references in the *Sketcher* mode.

6. On your own, create the 2D section as shown. The sketch consists of an **arc** (arc-center aligned to the origin) and a **horizontal line**. The line is connected to the two ends of the arc to form a closed region.

7. Modify the radius of the arc to **110 mm**.

8. On your own, use the **Blind Extrusion** option to create the feature. Note: set the depth of extrusion to **150** mm.

Creating a CUT Feature

❖   We will create a rectangular cut as the next solid feature.

1. In the Menu Manager window, select

    Feature → Create → Solid → Cut

2. In the **SOLID OPTS** submenu, confirm the **Extrude** and **Solid** options are highlighted, and then select **Done**.

3. In the **ATTRIBUTES** submenu, select

    One Side → Done

4. Pick the front semicircle of the model as the *sketching plane* and set DTM2 to point toward the **top** edge of the screen.

5. Use DTM1 and DTM2 to indicate the location of the rectangular cut.

6. Create a rectangle (**120 X 60 mm**) positioned as shown in the figure.

7. Complete cutout using the **Thru All** option.

Creating the CENTER_DRILL Feature

1. In the **Menu Manager** window, select

    Feature → Create → Solid → Hole

2. In the **Hole Type** section option, set the type to:
    Straight hole.

3. In the **Hole Placement** section, select the horizontal face of the last cut as the **primary reference**, the *placement plane*. (Hint: Click on the **Arrow** icon in front of the **primary reference** option to activate the selection.)

4. Select **DTM1** and **DTM3** as the two *linear references* and set the distances to **0.00** (press the **ENTER** key once after each input) as shown in the figure below.

5. In the **Hole Dimension** section, enter **20 mm** as the hole **Diameter**.

6. Set the **Depth One** option to **Variable** with a **Depth Value** of **55** and the **Depth Two** option to **None,** as shown in the above figure. (Note the corresponding direction symbols shown in the display area.)

7. Pick **Build feature** in the feature dialogue box to create the placed hole feature.

8. Select **Save** in the *Standard* toolbar.

9. In the message area, the message *"Enter object to save: U-BRACKET.PRT"* is displayed. Press the **ENTER** key or click on the **Accept** button to proceed with saving the completed model.

Examining the Parent/Child Relationships

The *Model Tree* window now contains seven items: three datum planes and four solid features. All of the parent/child relationships were established implicitly as we created the solid features. As more features are created, it becomes much more difficult to make a sketch showing all the parent/child relationships involved in the model. On the other hand, it is not really necessary to have a detailed picture showing all the relationships among the features. In using a feature-based modeler, the main emphasis is to consider the interactions that exist between the **immediate features**. Treat each feature as a unit by itself, and be clear on the parent/child relationships for each feature. Thinking in terms of features is what distinguishes *feature-based modeling* and the previous generation solid modeling techniques. Let us take a look at the last feature we created, the **CENTER_DRILL** feature. What are the parent/child relationships associated with this feature? (1) Since this is the last feature we created, it is not a parent feature to any other features. (2) Since we used one of the surfaces of the rectangular cutout as the sketching plane, the **RECT_CUT** feature is a parent feature to the **CENTER_DRILL** feature. (3) We also used DTM1 and DTM3 as sketching references; therefore, DTM1 and DTM3 are parents to the **CENTER_DRILL** feature.

Display Parent/Child Info

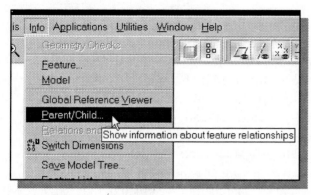

1. Select **Info** in the pull-down menus.

2. Pick the **Parent/Child** option. A pop-up menu appears.

3. Pick **CENTER_DRILL** in the *Model Tree* window.

❖ In the display area, DTM1, DTM3 and the **RECT_CUT** feature are displayed in the **Parents Of Current Feature** area; they are parents to the **CENTER_DRILL**. Note that there is no child listed in the **Children List** area; this is what we have expected since this is the last feature of the model.

4. Pick **Close** to return to the **Parent/Child** menu.

Modify a Parent Dimension

❖ Any changes to the parent features will affect the child feature. For example, if we modify the height of the **RECT_CUT** feature from 60 mm to 50 mm, the child feature (**CENTER_DRILL** feature) will be affected.

1. In the **PART MENU** window, select **Modify.**

2. Pick **RECT_CUT** in the *Model Tree* window.

3. Pick the vertical dimension text **60**.

4. Enter **50** in the message area.

5. Pick **Done** in the *Modify Menu* window.

6. Pick **Regenerate** in the **PART** menu window.

➢ The position of the **CENTER_DRILL** is moved downward by 10 mm since the placement plane is lowered by that amount; the drill does not go through the main body of the bracket anymore. If we are planing to make more dimensional changes to the rectangular cut, what would be your solution to make sure the drill will always go through the main body of the bracket?

7. On your own, adjust the height of the **RECT_CUT** feature to 60 mm or retrieve the saved version of the model.

8. On your own, adjust the depth of the **CENTER_DRILL** feature to **Thru All**.

A Design Change

> ➢ Engineering designs usually go through many revisions and changes. For example, a design change may call for a circular cutout instead of the current rectangular cutout feature in our model. *Pro/ENGINEER* provides an assortment of tools to handle design changes quickly and effectively. In the following sections, we will demonstrate some of the more advanced tools available in *Pro/ENGINEER*, which allow us to perform the modification of changing the rectangular cutout (120X60mm) to a circular cutout (radius 80 mm).

> ❖ Based on your knowledge of *Pro/ENGINEER* so far, how would you accomplish this modification? What other approaches can you think of that are also feasible? Of the approaches you came up with, which one is the easiest to do and which is the most flexible? If this design change were anticipated right at the beginning of the design process, what would be your choice in arranging the orders of the features? Take a few minutes to consider these questions and you are encouraged to perform the modifications prior to following through the rest of the tutorial.

> ➢ Before continuing to the next section, confirm the **U-Bracket** model is the same as what is shown on page 4-16.

Feature Suppression

❖ With *Pro/ENGINEER*, we can take several different approaches to accomplish this modification. We could (1) create a new model, or (2) change the shape of the existing cut feature using the ***Redefine*** command, or (3) perform **feature suppression** on the rectangular cut feature and add a circular cut feature. The third approach offers the most flexibility and requires the least amount of editing to the existing geometry. **Feature suppression** is a method that enables us to disable a feature while retaining the complete feature information; the feature can be reactivated at anytime. Prior to adding the new cut feature, we will first suppress the rectangular cut feature.

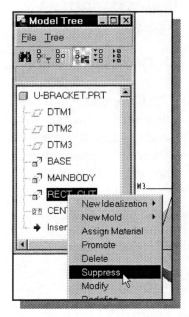

1. Move the cursor inside the *Model Tree* window. Push and hold the right-mouse-button on top of RECT_CUT. A pop-up menu is displayed.

2. Pick **Suppress** in the pop-up menu. A pop-up window is displayed.

➤ In the display area, notice both the **RECT_CUT** feature and the **CENTER_DRILL** feature are highlighted. The child feature cannot exist without its parent(s), and any modification to the parent (RECT_CUT) influence the child (CENTER_DRILL).

3. Pick **OK** in the pop-up window to confirm the suppression of the RECT_CUT and CENTER_DRILL features.

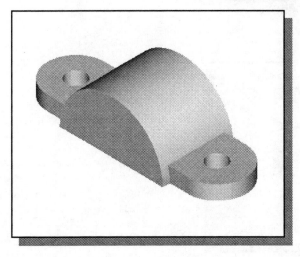

❖ We have literally ***gone back in time***. The RECT_CUT and CENTER_DRILL features have disappeared in the *Model Tree* window and the display area.

Creating the Circular Cut Feature

1. In the **Menu Manager** window, select

    Feature → Create → Solid → Cut

2. In the **SOLID OPTS** submenu, confirm the **Extrude** and **Solid** options are highlighted, and then select **Done**.

3. In the **ATTRIBUTES** submenu, select

    One Side → Done

4. Pick the front semicircle of the model as the *sketching plane* and set the *extrusion direction* to point toward the center of the model.

5. For the orientation of the sketching plane, select **DTM2** to point toward the **top** edge of the screen.

6. Accept **DTM1** and **DTM2** as the two references to position the location of the 2D sketch.

7. On your own, create a circle (diameter: **160 mm**), with the center aligned to the origin as shown in the figure below.

8. Complete cutout using the **Thru All** option.

Listing Suppressed Features

1. In the *Model Tree* window, click on the **Toggle display of items** button in the toolbar area as shown.

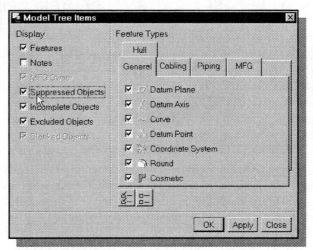

2. In the *Model Tree Items* window, click on the **Suppressed Objects** check-box to toggle on the display of suppressed features and components.

3. Click on the **OK** button to accept the settings.

❖ Notice in the *Model Tree* menu window a complete list of features is displayed. A small rectangular marker next to the feature signifies the feature is suppressed.

Suppressed features

Reactivate the CENTER_DRILL Feature

❖ To complete the model, we still need the **CENTER_DRILL** feature at the center. It is not necessary to duplicate the **CENTER_DRILL** feature that already exists in the database. We will reactivate the feature. This is called **Resume** in *Pro/ENGINEER*.

1. Move the cursor inside the *Model Tree* window. Click and hold the right-mouse-button on top of **CENTER_DRILL**. A pop-up menu is displayed.

2. Pick **Resume** in the pop-up menu.

➢ Notice that both of the suppressed features (**RECT_CUT** and **CENTER_DRILL**) are reactivated, again. *The child feature cannot exist without its parents.* All of the model's features are displayed in the display area and in the *Model Tree* window.

Reroute the CENTER_DRILL Feature

❖ In order to suppress only the RECT_CUT feature, we will need to remove the parent/child relationship that exists between RECT_CUT and CENTER_DRILL. The parent/child relationship was established when we used one of the RECT_CUT surfaces as the sketching plane. We will need to select a different sketching plane for the CENTER_DRILL feature. This is known as the **Reroute** operation in *Pro/ENGINEER*.

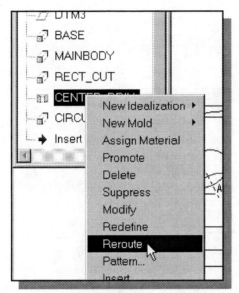

1. Move the cursor inside the *Model Tree* window. Click and hold the right-mouse-button on top of **CENTER_DRILL**. A pop-up menu is displayed.

2. Pick **Reroute** in the pop-up menu.

❖ The message "*Do you want to roll back the model?*" is displayed in the message area. The **Roll Back** option allows us to trace back in history and redefine the *sketching plane* and *reference planes* for the CENTER_DRILL feature.

3. Type **Yes** or pick the **Yes** icon in the message area.

4. We are now asked to redefine the ***placement plane*** for the **HOLE** feature. Pick **DTM2** in the display area.

5. After selecting the placement plane, we will be asked to redefine the **two position reference planes**. Pick **Same Ref** twice in the **REROUTE** menu.

❖ *Pro/ENGINEER* will regenerate the modified features and display the regenerated model. Everything looks the same, but RECT_CUT is no longer a parent feature to the CENTER_DRILL feature.

Suppress the RECT_CUT Feature

1. Move the cursor inside the *Model Tree* window. Click and hold the right-mouse-button on top of **RECT_CUT**. A pop-up menu is displayed.

2. Pick **Suppress** in the pop-up menu. A pop-up window is displayed.

3. Pick **OK** in the pop-up window to confirm the suppression of the RECT_CUT feature.

❖ Now, there is only one suppressed feature shown in the *Model Tree* window. We have successfully updated the model by switching off the RECT_CUT feature, but retained the complete feature information. On your own, do the design change that requires you to **suppress** the CIRCULAR_CUT feature and **resume** the RECT_CUT feature.

Questions:

1. How can we find out the order in which features are created in *Pro/ENGINEER*?

2. In *Pro/ENGINEER*, what does "rolling back the part" mean?

3. What is the difference between *redefining* and *rerouting*?

4. What determines how a feature reacts when other features in the model change?

5. Describe two methods in *Pro/ENGINEER* to access the **Redefine** feature command.

6. Create sketches showing the steps you plan to use to create the two models shown on the next page:

Ex.1)

Ex.2)

Exercises: (All dimensions are in inches.)

1. Plate thickness: 0.25 inches.

2. Base plate thickness: 0.25 inches. Boss height 0.5 inches.

3.

4.

Notes:

Lesson 5
Parametric Relations

Learning Objectives

When you have completed this lesson, you will be able to:
- ◆ **Create Parametric Relations.**
- ◆ **Use Dimensional Variables.**
- ◆ **Creating Sketch Files.**
- ◆ **Reuse 2-D sketches.**
- ◆ **Display and Modify Parametric Relations.**
- ◆ **Create Fully Constrained Sketches.**

Parametric Relations and Constraints

A primary and essential difference between parametric modeling and previous generation computer modeling is that parametric modeling captures the *design intent*. In the previous lessons, we have seen that the design philosophy of "*shape before size*" is implemented through the use of *Pro/ENGINEER's* **Intent Manager** and **Sketcher**. In performing geometric constructions, dimensional values are necessary to describe the **size** and **location** of constructed geometric entities. Besides using dimensions to define the geometry, we can also apply geometric rules to control geometric entities. More importantly, *Pro/ENGINEER* can capture design intent through the use of **geometric constraints**, **dimensional constraints**, and **parametric relations**. In *Pro/ENGINEER*, there are two types of constraints: **geometric constraints** and **dimensional constraints**. For part modeling in *Pro/ENGINEER*, constraints are applied to *2D sketches*. **Geometric constraints** are **geometric restrictions** that can be applied to geometric entities; for example, *horizontal*, *parallel*, *perpendicular*, and *tangent* are commonly used *geometric constraints* in parametric modeling. **Dimensional constraints** are used to describe the SIZE and LOCATION of individual geometric shapes. In *Pro/ENGINEER*, **parametric relations** are user-defined mathematical equations composed of *dimensional variables* and/or *design variables*. In parametric modeling, features are made of geometric entities with both relations and constraints describing individual design intent. In this lesson, we will discuss the use of parametric relations. More discussion on geometric constraints is covered in the next lesson.

Create a Simple Plate Design

- In parametric modeling, dimensions are design parameters that are used to control the sizes and locations of geometric features. Dimensions are more than just values; they can also be used as feature control variables. This concept is illustrated by the following example.

Using a Sketch file

1. Select the **Pro/ENGINEER** icon at the desktop or type [***proe***] at your system prompt to start *Pro/ENGINEER*. The *Pro/ENGINEER* main window will appear on the screen.

2. Pick the **Create New Object** icon in the toolbar. (We can also use the key combination **Ctrl-N** to start a new object.)

2. Pick *Create New Object*

3. In the *New* form, pick **Sketch** in the **Type** list.

4. Pick **OK** to accept the default filename (**s2d0001.sec**).

❖ The *Pro/ENGINEER Sketcher* appears. We have entered *Pro/ENGINEER's 2D Sketcher* mode directly. The concept of this option is to allow users to utilize *Pro/ENGINEER* in all aspects of the design process. In this case, we are using *Pro/ENGINEER* as a 2D sketching pad.

5. On your own, use the **Rectangle** and **Circle** commands and create a sketch as shown. (Do not be concerned with the dimensional values; we will adjust them in the following sections.)

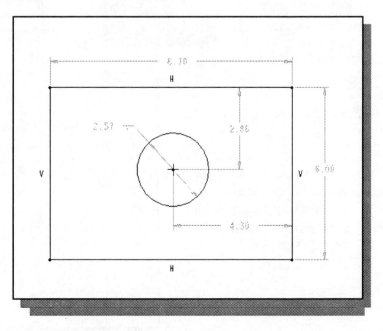

Dimensional Values and Dimensional Variables

❖ Initially in *Pro/ENGINEER*, dimensional values are used to reflect the size or distance between geometric entities created in the *Sketcher*. Each dimension is also assigned a name that allows the dimension to be used as a control variable. The default format is "**sdxx**," which stands for *Sketcher dimension* and the "**xx**" is a number that *Pro/ENGINEER* increments automatically.

Let us look at our current design, which represents a plate with a hole at the center. The dimensional values describe the size and/or location of the plate and the hole. If a modification is required to change the width of the plate, the location of the hole will remain the same as described by the two dimensional values. This is okay if that is the *design intent*. On the other hand, the *design intent* may require (1) keeping the hole at the center of the plate and (2) maintaining the size of the hole to be one-third of the height of the plate. We will establish a set of parametric relations using the dimensional variables to capture this design intent.

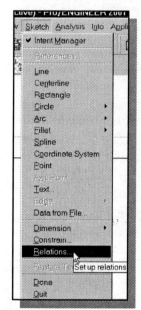

1. Pick **Relations** in the **Sketch** pull-down menu.

2. Pick **Add** in the **RELATIONS** submenu.

Pick *Add*

❖ Notice in the display area the *dimensional variables* are displayed instead of the *dimensional values*. (The dimensional variables are in the **sdxx** format, which represents the dimensions are *2D Sketcher* dimensions.)

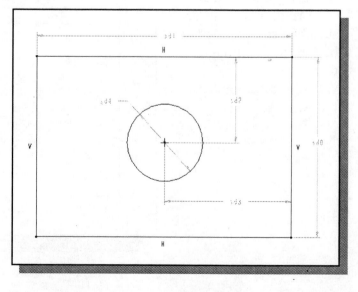

❖ In the message area, *Pro/ENGINEER* expects us to input mathematical equations.

3. Enter **sd3=sd1/2** as the first equation. This equation sets the horizontal dimension for the location of the hole (**sd3**) to be one-half of the width of the rectangle (**sd1**). The variable names on your sketch might be different than what is displayed here. Use the corresponding variable names to establish the parametric relation.

4. Pick Accept to confirm the equation entered.

4. Click on the "check mark" icon to accept the entered equation.

5. Enter **sd2=sd0/2** as the second equation. This equation makes sure the vertical dimension for the location of the hole (**sd2**) will always be one-half of the height of the rectangle (**sd0**). The variable names on your sketch might be different than what is displayed here. Use the corresponding variable names to establish the parametric relation.

6. Click the "check mark" icon to accept the entered equation.

7. Enter **sd4=sd0/3** as the third equation. This equation sets the size of the hole (**sd4**) to be always one-third of the height of the rectangle (**sd0**). The variable names on your sketch might be different than what is displayed here. Use the corresponding variable names to establish the parametric relation.

8. Click the "check mark" icon to accept the entered equation.

9. Press the **ENTER** key without typing any equation. This will end the **Add Relations** command.

10. Pick **Switch Dim** in the **RELATIONS** submenu.

❖ Note the dimensions are automatically adjusted using the relations entered.

11. On your own, modify the width of the rectangle to **8**, and the height of the rectangle to **6**.

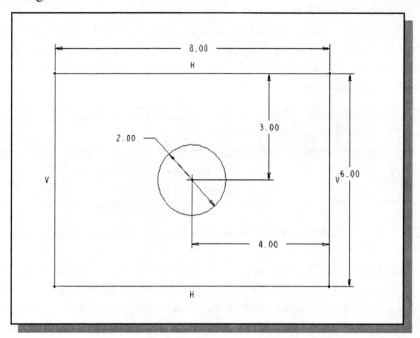

12. On your own, modify the width of the rectangle to **10**, and the height of the rectangle to **7.5**.

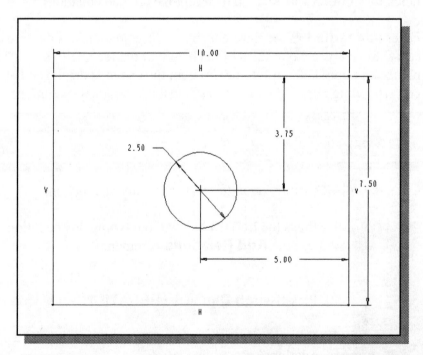

❖ *Pro/ENGINEER* automatically adjusts the dimensions of the design, and the parametric relations we entered are also applied and maintained. The dimensional constraints are used to control the size and location of the hole. The design intent, previously expressed by statements (1) and (2) at the beginning of this section, is now embedded into the model.

Save the Sketch File and Exit the Sketcher Mode

1. From the icon panel, select the **Save** icon. You can also use **Ctrl-S** to save the model.

2. Click on the **Accept value** button or hit the **ENTER** key to accept the filename and proceed to save the file.

3. Pick **Done** in the **SKETCHER** menu to exit *Pro/ENGINEER Sketcher* mode.

Sketch Files vs. Part Files

The main advantage of creating sketch files is that we do not need to go through all the steps that are required for part files in order to create 2D sketches in *Pro/ENGINEER*. The Pro/*ENGINEER Sketcher* can be viewed as the equivalent of the designer's sketchpad. Sketch files can be used to create rough sketches during the initial design stage. Modifications and changes can be done quickly and effectively without worrying about the interactions between features or parts. The use of sketch files allows us to concentrate on one feature at a time.

Once the sketches are finalized, we can then incorporate the finalized sketches into any part file. This approach allows us to reuse any of the 2D sketches that have been created. Note that *Pro/ENGINEER* also allows us to export any of the 2D sketches that we have created in any part file. In fact, each time we entered the *2D Sketcher*, Pro/ENGINEER created a sketch file automatically. The automatically generated sketch file is discarded when we exit *Pro/ENGINEER* or when we issue the **Erase** command.

In the following section, we will illustrate the procedure for incorporating an existing sketch from a sketch file into a part model, so that the 2D sketch can be used to create a solid feature.

Starting a new *Pro/ENGINEER* Part

1. Select **File** in the pull-down menus. Pick the **New** option. Notice that we can also use the key combination **Ctrl-N** to start a new object.

2. In the *New* form, enter **Plate** as the solid part file **Name**.

❖ Note the **Use default template** option is switched *on*. A template file is a regular part file that contains some of the initial settings defined.

3. Pick **OK** to continue. A set of predefined features, three datum planes and a *coordinate system*, appear on the screen.

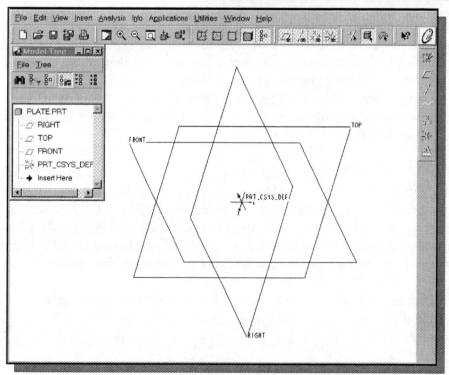

Creating the Base Feature

1. In the Menu Manager window, select

    Feature → Create → Solid → Protrusion

2. In the **SOLID OPTS** submenu, confirm the **Extrude** and **Solid** options are highlighted, and then select **Done**.

    Extrude → Solid → Done

❖ The protrusion's feature dialog box appears on the screen. We will need to define all elements listed to complete the feature.

3. In the **ATTRIBUTES** submenu, select

    One Side → Done

Pick *One Side*

Pick *Done*

4. We will use datum plane **Front** as the sketch plane. Use the left-mouse-button and select **Front** in the *Model Tree* window.

5. Confirm the viewing direction of the sketching plane as shown. Pick **Okay** in the Menu Manager window.

6. In the **SKET VIEW** submenu, pick **Right**.

6. Pick *Right*

7. In the *Model Tree* window, pick datum plane **Right**.

7. Pick *Right*

Placing the 2D Sketch

1. We will accept the default selection of the two datum planes, **Right** and **Top,** as the references for the 2D sketch.

2. Toggle *off* the **Intent Manager** option by selecting through the **Sketch** pull-down menu as shown.

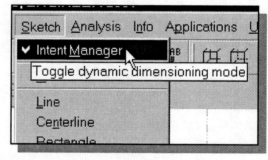

3. Pick **Sec Tools** in the **SKETCHER** menu.

4. Pick **Place Section** in the **SEC TOOLS** submenu.

5. In the *Open* form, select **s2d0001.sec** in the file list.

6. Pick **Open** to proceed with importing the 2D sketch into the current model file.

❖ A **section sub-window** showing the sketch appears on the screen.

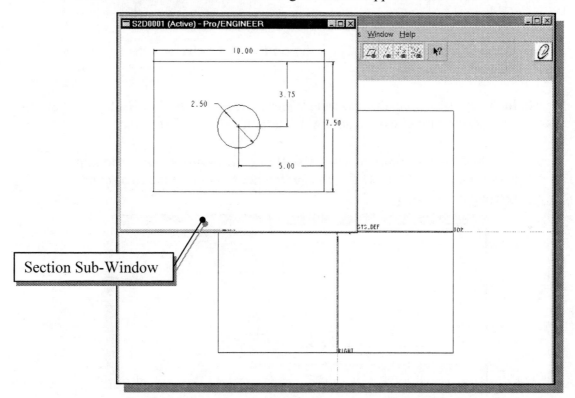

Section Sub-Window

7. In the message area, the message *"Enter rotating angle, press <ESC> for another section (0.0000)"* is displayed. Click on the **Accept value** button to accept the default value.

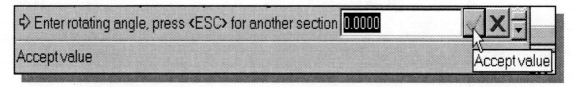

8. In the *Section* sub-window, pick the **top-left corner** as the *scaling origin*.

9. In the *Section* sub-window, pick the **center of the circle** as the *point to move for scale/drag.*

10. In the message area, the message *"Enter a scaling factor"* is displayed. Pick the "**check mark**" icon to accept the default value (**1.00**).

11. Use the *Dynamic Zoom* function ([**Ctrl**] + [**left-mouse-button**]) to adjust the zoom scale. Place the 2D sketch near the intersection of the two selected references as shown.

➢ If your placement is not exactly aligned, the message "*Should the highlighted entities be aligned?*" will display in the message area. *Pro/ENGINEER* will try to align the selected point on the 2D sketch to the two references. Pick **Align** in the **Query** submenu to confirm aligning the center of the circle to the references.

We have successfully transferred in the 2D sketch done previously. We remain in the *Pro/ENGINEER Sketcher* as if we had just created the 2D sketch by using the **Rectangle** and **Circle** commands. The set of parametric relations we have established in the sketch file is also transferred into the part file.

Display the Parametric Relations

1. Pick **Relation** in the **SKETCHER** menu.

2. Pick **Show Rel** in the **RELATIONS** submenu.

- An information window appears and the defined parametric equations are displayed. Note that the parametric relations are imported and maintained, but *Pro/ENGINEER* has automatically reassigned the variable names.

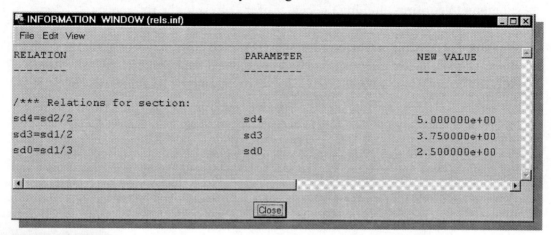

3. Pick **Close** to return to the **SKETCHER** menu.

4. Select **Switch Dim** in the **RELATIONS** submenu to redisplay the dimension values.

❖ On your own, modify the overall width of the rectangle to **8** to confirm the parametric relations are maintained. Reset the value back to **10** before continuing to the next section. (Hint: Use the **Modify → Regenerate** commands in the *Sketcher* menu.)

5. Select **Regenerate** in the **SKETCHER** menu. In the message area, the message "*Section regenerated successfully*" is displayed. *Pro/ENGINEER* has examined the 2D sketch and confirmed the sketch is fully defined.

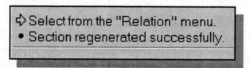

❖ Note that with the *Intent Manager* switched on, *Pro/ENGINEER* will automatically maintain a *fully defined sketched geometry* as the sketch is made. Since we have switched off the *Intent Manager* option, we will need to use the **Regenerate** command to have *Pro/ENGINEER* confirm the 2D sketch is fully defined.

6. Select **Done** in the **SKETCHER** menu to accept the created section and exit the *2D Sketcher*.

Complete the Extrusion Feature

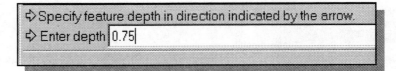

1. The **Blind** option allows us to enter the depth value of the extrusion. Pick **Done** in the **Menu Manager** window to proceed.

2. In the message area, enter **0.75** as the depth of extrusion.

3. Pick **OK** in the feature dialogue box to create the solid.

4. On your own, use the *Dynamic Viewing* function ([**Ctrl**] + [middle-mouse-button]) to view the 3D model.

Edit Parametric Relations

❖ Once the model is constructed, there are several methods to modify the existing parametric relations and/or create new parametric relations.

(a) Modify through [Menu Manager → Feature]

1. In the **PART** menu window, select

   Feature → Redefine

2. In the display window, pick any **edge** of the plate.

3. Pick **Section** in the *Extrude* dialogue box.

4. Pick **Define** in the *Extrude* dialogue box.

5. Pick **Sketch** in the **SECTION** submenu.

6. We have gone back into the *Pro/ENGINEER Sketcher*.

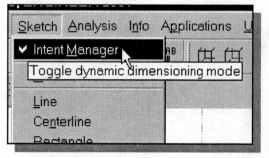

7. Toggle *off* the *Intent Manager* option by selecting through the **Sketch** pull-down menu as shown.

8. Pick **Relation** in the **SKETCHER** menu.

9. Pick **Edit Rel** in the **RELATIONS** submenu.

10. In the *text editor* window, enter the comment lines as shown. (The lines that begin with **/*** are treated as comments.)

Add **/*** in front of this equation

```
/* Hole centered horizontally
sd4=sd2/2
/* Hole centered vertically
/* sd3=sd1/2
/* Hole Size
sd0=sd1/3
```

11. Pick **Save** in the **File** pull-down menu to save the changes.

12. On your own, **Exit** the text editor.

13. Select **Switch Dim** in the **RELATIONS** submenu to redisplay the dimension values.

14. Pick **Modify** in the **SKETCHER** menu.

15. Select the *height dimension of the rectangle* with the left-mouse-button; the current dimension value is displayed as 7.50 on the screen.

16. Change the height of the plate to **10**.

17. Pick **Regenerate** in the **SKETCHER** menu.

18. Pick **Done** in the **SKETCHER** menu to exit the *Pro/ENGINEER Sketcher*.

19. Pick **OK** in the *Extrude* dialogue box. The parametric relations are maintained and the design appears as shown in the figure below.

(b) Modify through [Model Tree Window]

1. Move the cursor inside the *Model Tree* window. Click and hold the right-mouse-button on top of the solid feature, the last feature in the model tree window. A pop-up menu is displayed.

2. Pick **Redefine** in the pop-up menu.

❖ The *Extrude* dialogue box appears on the screen, similar to selecting **Redefine** through the **Menu Manager**, and we can access any elements relating to the feature, including the **Edit Rel** option.

3. On your own, edit the equation as shown in the figure below. We will also add a relation to control the height of the plate (equal to one-half of the width of the plate.)

Reactivate this equation

Add relation

4. On your own, **Save** the changes and **Exit** the text editor.

5. Pick **Modify** in the **SKETCHER** menu.

6. Select the *width dimension of the rectangle* with the left-mouse-button; the current dimension value is displayed as **10** on the screen.

7. Change the width of the plate to **12**.

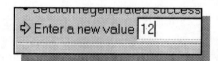

8. Pick **Regenerate** in the **SKETCHER** menu.

9. Pick **Done** in the **SKETCHER** menu to exit the *Pro/ENGINEER Sketcher*.

10. Pick **OK** in the *Extrude* dialogue box. The parametric relations are maintained and the design appears as shown in the below figure.

(c) Modify through [Menu manager → Part]

1. In the **PART** menu window, select **Relations**.

2. Pick **Feat Rel** in the **MODEL REL** menu.

3. Pick the **plate** feature in the *Model Tree* window.

4. Pick **Section** in the **FEAT REL** submenu.

5. Pick **Edit Rel** in the **RELATIONS** submenu.

6. In the text editor, change the *hole size* to **one-half** of the height of the plate.

7. On your own, **Save** the changes and **Exit** the text editor.

8. Pick **Done** in the **MODEL REL** submenu.

9. Pick **Regenerate** in the **PART** menu.

Feature Relations

In *Pro/ENGINEER*, **parametric relations** can be defined within a part or among parts of an assembly. So far, we have demonstrated the use of parametric **section relations**, which are applied to the 2D sketch within a feature. Similar procedures can also be applied to the feature, part, and assembly levels to establish parametric relations.

In part files, we can establish three types of **parametric relations**:

*   **Part Relations** relate different feature parameters to each other in a single model.

*   **Feature Relations** relate specific parameters within one feature in the model. A feature relation can be for the 2D sketch only or for the entire feature.

*   **Pattern Relations** relate specific parameters within a pattern in the model.

1. In the **PART** menu window, select **Relations**.

2. Pick **Part Rel** in the **MODEL REL** menu.

3. Pick any edge of the solid model in the graphics window.

4. Pick **Add** in the **RELATIONS** submenu.

5. In the message area, *Pro/ENGINEER* expects us to input mathematical equations. Enter **d5=d1/6**, where **d5** is the depth of extrusion and **d1** is the height dimension of the plate. The variable names on your screen might be different than what is displayed here. Use the corresponding variable names to establish the parametric relation.

6. Pick the "check mark" icon to accept the entered equation.

7. Press the **ENTER** key without typing any equation. This will end the Add Relations command.

8. Pick **Done** in the **MODEL REL** submenu.

9. Pick **Regenerate** in the **PART** menu.

❖ The thickness of the part is updated based on the parametric equation we entered. The parametric relations are maintained by the system so that an intelligent part is created.

Questions:

1. What is the difference between *dimensional values* and *dimensional variables*?

2. What is the easiest way to modify existing parametric relations?

3. How do we display the *dimensional variable* names?

4. Describe the three types of **parametric relations** available in *Pro/ENGINEER*.

5. How do we create parametric relations in *Pro/ENGINEER*?

6. Describe two different methods to modify existing parametric relations.

7. Create binary tree sketches showing the steps you plan to use to create the two models shown on the next page:

Ex.1)

Ex.2)

Exercises:

(Establish three parametric relations for each of the designs and experiment with the different modification techniques illustrated in this lesson.)

1. Dimensions are in inches.

2. Dimensions are in inches.

3.   Dimensions are in inches. Plate thickness: 0.25 inches.

Notes:

Lesson 6
Geometric Construction Tools

Learning Objectives

When you have completed this lesson, you will be able to:
- **Use the Trim/Extend command.**
- **Use the Offset command.**
- **Understand the Profile Sketch Approach.**
- **Use the 2-D Fillet command.**
- **Duplicate geometry using the Copy & Paste Option.**
- **Use the Projected Geometry Command to Reuse Sketches.**
- **Edit using Click and Drag.**

Introduction

The main characteristics of solid modeling are the accuracy and completeness of the geometric database of the three-dimensional objects. However, working in three-dimensional space using input and output devices that are largely two-dimensional in nature is potentially tedious and confusing. The ***Pro/ENGINEER 2D Sketcher*** provides an assortment of two-dimensional construction tools to make the creation of 2D geometry easier and more efficient.

In doing geometric constructions, dimensional values are necessary to describe the **SIZE** and **LOCATION** of constructed geometric entities. Besides using dimensions to define the geometry, we can also apply geometric rules to control geometric entities. This set of geometric rules is known as **geometric constraints** in parametric modeling. The geometric constraints are **geometric restrictions** that can be applied to geometric entities, such as tangent, parallel, perpendicular, etc. In parametric modeling, features are made of geometric entities with **parametric relations** and **geometric constraints** describing individual design intent. In this lesson, we will discuss the use of *Pro/ENGINEER Sketcher's* geometric construction tools, including the application of **geometric constraints**.

The Gasket Design

All Dimensions are in mm.

❖ Based on your knowledge of *Pro/ENGINEER* so far, how would you create this design? What are the more difficult geometry involved in the design? Take a few minutes to consider a modeling strategy and do preliminary planning by sketching on a piece of paper. You are also encouraged to create the design on your own prior to following through the tutorial.

Modeling Strategy

Starting *Pro/ENGINEER*

1. Select the **Pro/ENGINEER** icon at the desktop or type [*proe*] at your system prompt to start *Pro/ENGINEER*. The *Pro/ENGINEER* main window will appear on the screen.

2. Pick the **New Object** icon in the toolbar. (We can also use the key combination **Ctrl-N** to start a new object.)

2. Pick *Create New Object*

Enter *Gasket*

3. In the *New* form, enter **Gasket** as the solid part file **Name**.

4. Switch *off* the use of the **Default Template Option**.

5. Pick **OK** to continue. The *Model Tree* window and the **Menu Manager** window appear on the screen.

6. In the *New File Options* window, select **mmns_part_solid** as the template to use. This will set up the **System Units** to **millimeter Newton Second**.

❖ A set of datum planes, datum axes and units are set up using the selected template.

Using the 2D Sketcher in 3D Orientation

1. Select **Utilities** in the pull-down menu.

2. Pick **Environment** in the pull-down list.

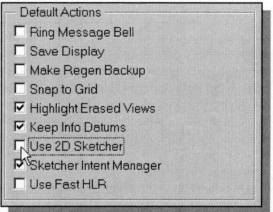

3. Toggle *off* the **Use 2D Sketcher** option. The **Use 2D Sketcher** option determines if the sketching plane will be oriented to the computer screen or will remain in the default view angle.

4. Pick **OK** to exit the *Environment* form.

Creating the Base Feature

1. In the **Menu Manager** window, select

Feature → Create → Solid → Protrusion

2. In the **SOLID OPTS** submenu, confirm the **Extrude** and **Solid** options are highlighted, and then select **Done**.

Extrude → Solid → Done

❖ The protrusion's feature dialog box appears on the screen. We will need to define all elements listed to complete the feature.

3. In the **ATTRIBUTES** submenu, select

   One Side → Done

   Pick *One Side*

   Pick *Done*

4. We will use datum plane **Front** as the sketch plane. Use the left-mouse-button and select **Front** in the *Model Tree* window.

5. Confirm the direction of viewing the sketching plane as shown. Pick **Okay** in the Menu Manager window.

6. In the **SKET VIEW** submenu, pick **Right**.

   6. Pick *Right*

7. In the *Model Tree* window, pick **Right**.

   7. Pick *Right*

❖ Note that the display of the datum planes remains in the 3D orientation. The **Use 2D Sketcher** option was turned *off* and the sketching plane remains in the default view angle. In most cases, orienting the sketching plane to the computer screen simplifies the construction of 2D sketches.

2D Sketching

1. Accept the default selection of the two datum planes, **Right** and **Top**, as the references for the 2D sketch by clicking the **Close** button.

2. On your own, use the *Dynamic Rotation* quick key ([Ctrl]+[middle-mouse-button]) and view the established datum planes and axes. Note the different colors associated with the two sides of each datum plane. Each surface in *Pro/ENGINEER* has a positive side and a negative side.

3. Pick **Sketch View** in the **Sketcher** menu. This will align the sketching plane to the computer screen. Also note the four display-control icons to the right side of the **Sketch View** icon.

4. Move the graphics cursor to the **Line** icon in the *Sketcher* toolbar. A *help-tip* box appears next to the cursor and a brief description of the command options is displayed in the message area.

5. Switch *on* the grid display and create the geometry with the geometric constraints shown, by selecting points near the grid-points indicated.

❖ Do not end the Line command. We will continue to sketch after the following discussion of the implicit geometric relationships.

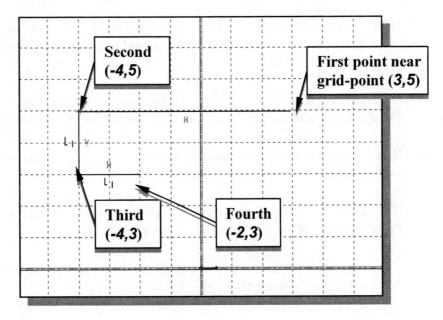

❖ Note that the *Intent Manager* displays different constraint symbols to show perpendicularities, verticals, equal length, etc. The three geometric constraint symbols shown on the screen represent three types of geometric constraints: *vertical, horizontal* and *equal length.*

V   Vertical   indicates a segment is vertical

H   Horizontal   indicates a segment is horizontal

L   Equal Length   indicates two segments are of equal length

Implicit Geometric Relationships

In parametric modeling software, such as *Pro/ENGINEER*, **geometric constraints** can be applied to geometric entities to ensure the shape of a part behaves predictably as changes are made. By default, *Pro/ENGINEER* automatically adds constraints to geometry as they are constructed. The following is a list of assumptions about geometric relationships in *Pro/ENGINEER* sketches.

- **If the sketched lines are approximately horizontal or vertical, *Pro/ENGINEER* makes them exactly horizontal or vertical.**

- **If the sketched lines are approximately parallel or perpendicular, *Pro/ENGINEER* makes them exactly parallel or perpendicular.**

- **If the sketched lines are approximately equal to the length of an existing line, *Pro/ENGINEER* makes them equal to the length of the existing line.**

- **If the sketched arcs or circles are approximately equal to the radius of an existing arc or circle, *Pro/ENGINEER* makes them equal to the radius of the existing arc or circle.**

- **If the sketched entities are approximately symmetrical about a centerline, *Pro/ENGINEER* makes them symmetrical about the centerline.**

- **If the sketched entities are approximately tangent to each other, *Pro/ENGINEER* makes them tangent to each other.**

- **If the sketched entities are approximately collinear to each other, *Pro/ENGINEER* makes them collinear to each other.**

- **If the sketched endpoints are approximately on other entities, *Pro/ENGINEER* makes them exactly on the entities.**

Note that we can override these implicit rules by adding appropriate dimensions and/or geometric constraints. We can also disable the implicit constraints during geometric constructions. A single click of the right-mouse-button (in the display area) will toggle on/off the displayed constraint. We can always modify the constraints to ensure the design intent.

A good rule of thumb to follow in using an implicit-geometric-constraint-based modeler, such as *Pro/ENGINEER*, is to exaggerate the feature during the initial sketch. For example, if we want to create an angle between two lines, we should exaggerate when sketching (that is, sketch an eighty-five degree angle at sixty degrees) so that *Pro/ENGINEER* will not make them perpendicular.

Disable/Enable Constraints

Geometric constraints can be modified while sketching; the rules to **disable** or **enable** constraints are as follows:
- The current constraint is highlighted in red.
- Disable the current constraint by pressing the **right-mouse-button**. To enable it again, press the **right-mouse-button** again.
- Lock in the current constraint by holding the [**SHIFT**] key and pressing the **right-mouse-button**. To unlock the constraint, press the [**SHIFT**] key and the **right-mouse-button** again.
- When more than one constraint is active, you can walk through them all by using the [**TAB**] key. Each one will be made current in turn, and can then be disabled or locked.

We will next demonstrate the usage of the rules in the current sketch.

1. Move the cursor below the last endpoint we created, near grid point (**-2,3**); click the **right-mouse-button** once when the **vertical** and **equal length** constraint symbols are displayed. The right-mouse-click disables the current constraint, the *equal length constraint* in this case.

2. Hit the [**TAB**] key once and click the **right-mouse-button** once. Both of the constraint symbols are displayed with an inclined line to signify the constraints have been disabled.

3. Click the **right-mouse-button** again and the current constraint, the *vertical constraint*, is enabled.

4. Hit the **[TAB]** key once and click the right-mouse-button again. Both of the constraints are reactivated.

5. Move the cursor near the horizontal axis (datum plane **TOP**). Notice the cursor will *SNAP* on to the horizontal axis.

6. Pick near grid point **(-1.5,0)** and create an inclined line as shown.

7. Pick near grid point **(4,0)** to create a horizontal line on the horizontal axis.

Sixth point: near grid point (*4,0*)

8. In the display area, click the **middle-mouse-button** once to end the Line command.

❖ Notice that dimensions are added automatically to describe the locations of the lines.

Create and Divide a Circle

1. In the *Sketcher* toolbar, select **Circle** as shown. The default option is to create a circle by specifying the center point and a point through which the circle will pass.

2. Place the center of the circle toward the right side of the sketch, approximately at grid point (**5,5**).

3. Pick near the right endpoint (**3,5**) of the top horizontal line; an implicit alignment constraint will applied automatically.

4. In the *Sketcher* toolbar, activate the **Divide** command by selecting the icon in the icon stack.

First point

Second point

5. Click on the lower portion of the circle at two locations to divide the circle into two arcs, as shown in the figure.

6. Click once with the middle-mouse-button to end the command.

❖ Note the *Intent Manager* automatically added additional dimensions as the circle is divided into two arcs.

7. Select the lower arc by clicking with the **left-mouse-button**. Notice the selected entity is highlighted.

8. Inside the graphics area, press down the right-mouse-button to display the option menu and select **Delete** as shown.

Create a closed region Sketch

1. Pick **Line** in the *Sketcher* toolbar.

2. Pick the right-endpoint of the lower horizontal line to attach the first endpoint of the new line.

3. Move the cursor along the arc and note that different types of constraints are feasible at different locations. Attach the end of the line to the end of the arc. (Note that a *tangent* constraint may be applied automatically depending upon the size of the arc you have created.)

4. Inside the display area, click the **middle-mouse-button** once to end the Line command.

❖ Note the *Intent Manager* automatically adds and removes additional dimensions and/or constraints to maintain a fully described sketch.

Modify Geometry by Drag-and-Drop

- In *Pro/ENGINEER*, geometric entities can also be modified by *drag-and-drop* with the left-mouse-button. Note that the applied geometric constraints, such as vertical or horizontal, are maintained by the system during the editing.

1. Click on the **Model Tree display** icon to switch *off* the *Model Tree* display.

2. Click on the **Dimensions display** icon to switch *off* the display of the dimensions. Note the other display icons available in the *Standard* toolbar area.

3. Click on the **Select** icon in the *Sketcher* toolbar.

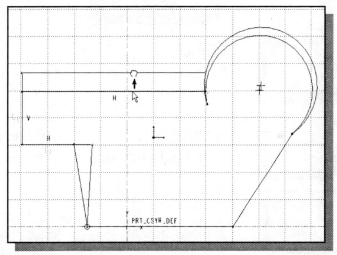

4. Use the left-mouse-button to drag the top-horizontal line upward and notice that the geometry is adjusted while maintaining the applied geometric constraints.

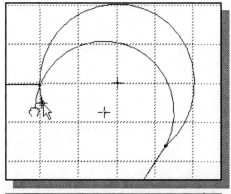

5. On your own, experiment with adjusting the locations of the endpoint of the arc, the center point of the arc, etc.

- We can dynamically modify geometric entities using drag-and-drop. The drag-and-drop capabilities provide a more flexible modeling environment especially when exact dimension values are not known.

6. Click on the **Dimensions display** icon to switch *on* the display of the dimensions.

Controlling Geometric Relationships

❖ In *Pro/ENGINEER*, a set of rules can be applied to geometric entities to ensure the capture of the design intent. This set of rules is called the **geometric constraints**. As we create geometric entities such as lines and circles in the *Sketcher* mode, the *Intent Manager* automatically add dimensions and/or geometric constraints. The application of different constraints will affect the geometry differently, and the design intent can be embedded into the model file through the proper use of constraints.

1. Pick **Constraints** in the *Sketcher* toolbar.

❖ The **Constraints** submenu appears on the screen. Note that the nine constraint icons actually provide more than a dozen of the applicable constraint options.

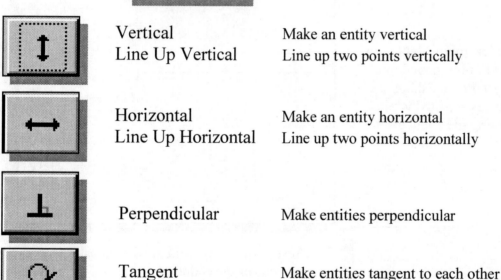

| Vertical | Make an entity vertical |
| Line Up Vertical | Line up two points vertically |

| Horizontal | Make an entity horizontal |
| Line Up Horizontal | Line up two points horizontally |

| Perpendicular | Make entities perpendicular |

| Tangent | Make entities tangent to each other |

| Midpoint | Place point on the middle of the line |

Collinear	Make two lines collinear
Point On Entity	Move a point on entity
Same Points	Make two points coincident

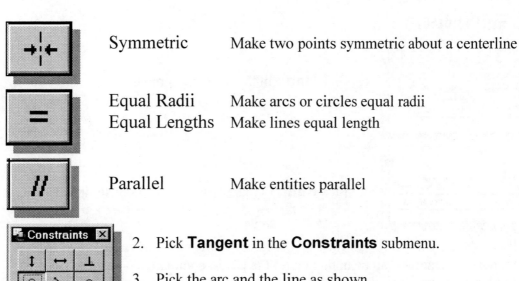

	Symmetric	Make two points symmetric about a centerline
	Equal Radii	Make arcs or circles equal radii
	Equal Lengths	Make lines equal length
	Parallel	Make entities parallel

2. Pick **Tangent** in the **Constraints** submenu.

3. Pick the arc and the line as shown.

Pick these two entities

❖ Note that *Pro/ENGINEER* adjusts the two entities to satisfy the applied tangent constraint.

4. Pick **Vertical** in the **Constraints** submenu.

5. Pick the inclined line on the left. Notice the **vertical symbol** is displayed as the constraint is applied.

REDO and UNDO

1. Pick **Undo** in the *Sketcher* toolbar.

2. Pick **Redo** to reapply the vertical constraint.

❖ *Pro/ENGINEER* records all the steps used while we are in *Sketcher* mode. All *Sketcher* operations can be undone with the Undo command. We can use **Undo** and **Redo** to experiment with different designs we have in mind.

3. In the *Sketcher* toolbar, select **Fillet**.

4. The Fillet command allows us to create a fillet by picking two intersecting entities. Create the three fillets as shown.

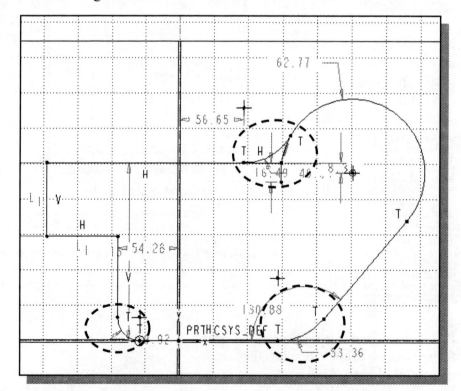

❖ Note that in *Pro/ENGINEER*, the Fillet command automatically trims two lines and creates break points when arcs or circles are involved.

5. On your own, **Delete** the two extra segments near the top fillet.

Using Sketcher Points

We will next create a *Sketcher* **Point** to define the theoretical intersection of two lines; the point can then be used for dimensioning purposes.

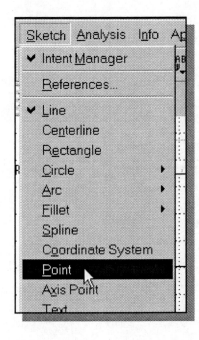

1. Select **Point** in the **Sketch** pull-down menu.

2. Move the cursor near the lower right corner of the sketch. Place the point so that it is aligned to the inclined line as shown.

3. On your own, use the **Line Up Horizontal** option to align the center of the top arc and the top left corner of the sketch.

4. On your own, use the **Equal Radii** option to make the two lower arcs equal radii.

5. Use the Dimension command and add the two dimensions as shown.

Deleting Geometric Constraints

1. Choose **Select** in the *Sketcher* toolbar.

2. Pick one of the equal length symbols (**L1**).

3. Press and hold down the right-mouse-button to display the option menu and select **Delete** to remove the *equal length constraint*.

❖   Notice *Pro/ENGINEER* removed the equal length constraint and a horizontal dimension is added to the sketched section.

❖   In *Pro/ENGINEER*, completed 2D sketches (**sections**) are always fully constrained. *Pro/ENGINEER's Intent Manager* incorporates the **Dynamic Dimensioning** feature, which means that *Sketcher* adds or removes dimensions and constraints *on the fly* to keep sections fully constrained, even in the middle of sketching. *Dynamic Dimensioning* occurs during all *Sketcher* operations. 2D sections are never under-dimensioned or over-dimensioned.

Weak Dimensions and Constraints

❖ Dimensions and constraints are called "*weak*" if *Pro/ENGINEER Sketcher* can remove them without any confirmation from us. All dimensions added dynamically by *Sketcher* are *weak*, as are many of the constraints. Weak dimensions and constraints appear gray.

There is no need to remove undesired weak dimensions and constraints explicitly. Instead, simply add the desired dimensions and constraints. The weak ones will be removed automatically as appropriate.

If you attempt to add a constraint or dimension that conflicts with other *strong* dimensions or constraints, the conflicting items will immediately be highlighted and you will be prompted to select one or more of them to be removed. This keeps the section from ever becoming over-constrained or over-dimensioned.

• Weak constraints and dimensions can be "*strengthened*" by choosing **Strong** in the popup option menu. This will ensure that they are never removed without confirmation. Modifying weak dimensions also strengthens them.

➢ On your own, create/strengthen additional dimensions so that the sketch appears as shown in the figure below. (Do not be overly concerned with the dimension values; concentrate on applying proper constraints and dimensions.)

Completing the Base Feature

1. On your own, adjust the dimensions as shown in the figure below.

2. In the *Sketcher* toolbar, click on the **Accept** icon to end the *Pro/ENGINEER 2D Sketcher* and proceed to the next element of the feature definition.

3. In the **Spec To** submenu, confirm **Blind** is highlighted as shown. Click on **Done** to proceed with the blind extrusion option.

4. In the message area, enter **5** as the extrusion depth.

5. Pick **OK** in the feature dialogue box to create the solid.

➢ On your own, use the *Dynamic Viewing* function ([**Ctrl**] + [middle-mouse-button]) to view the 3D solid model.

Using the Offset Loop Option to create a CUT feature

1. In the **Menu Manager** window, select

Feature → Create → Solid → Cut

2. In the **SOLID OPTS** submenu, confirm the **Extrude** and **Solid** options are highlighted, and then select **Done**.

Extrude → Solid → Done

3. Select **Done** in the **ATTRIBUTES** submenu.

4. Pick the front face of the solid model as the sketching plane and set the cut direction into the solid model.

5. On your own, use the **RIGHT** datum plane as the *reference plane* oriented toward the **right** edge of the computer screen.

6. Accept using the **RIGHT** and **TOP** datum planes as sketching references.

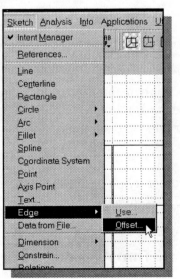

7. In the **Sketch** pull-down menu, select

Edge → Offset

8. Choose **Loop** in the **Type** menu as shown.

9. Click on the inside of the front surface of the base feature. The contour of the surface is automatically selected. An arrowhead is displayed pointing away from the center of the base feature.

10. The message "*Enter offset in the direction of the arrow*" is displayed in the message area. Enter **-15**. The negative sign will place the offset curve on the inside of the base feature.

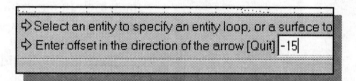

⇨ Select an entity to specify an entity loop, or a surface to
⇨ Enter offset in the direction of the arrow [Quit] -15

11. Click the **Close** button to accept the created offset geometry.

➢ Notice there is only the offset dimension needed to define the geometry. The **Offset Edge** command creates parent/child relationships with the referenced feature. The offset entities are updated automatically as the base geometry is modified.

12. In the *Sketcher* toolbar, click on the **Accept** icon to end the *Pro/ENGINEER 2D Sketcher* and proceed to the next element of the feature definition.

13. On your own, use the **Thru All** option and complete the offset cut feature.

➢ Use the *Dynamic Viewing* function ([Ctrl] + [middle-mouse-button]) to view the 3D model.

➢ On your own, modify the design by creating two additional fillets on the inside left corner as shown in the below figure.

All Dimensions are in mm.

Dynamically Modify the thickness of the design

• We can dynamically modify feature sections using the same drag-and-drop capability available in the *Intent Manager*. The drag-and-drop capabilities provide us a very flexible modeling environment, which can be quite useful during the conceptual design stage of a product.

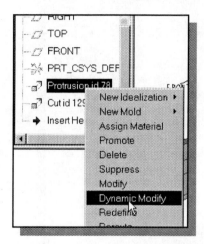

1. Move the cursor inside the *Model Tree* window. Click once with the right-mouse-button on top of the base solid feature, the first solid feature created. A pop-up menu is displayed.

2. Pick **Dynamic Modify** in the pop-up menu.

3. A rectangular marker appears near the center of the feature. Move the cursor near the marker and the pointer symbol changes to a hand, allowing us to drag entities to a new location.

4. Drag with the left-mouse-button to increase the thickness of the design.

5. Click once with the middle-mouse-button to accept the modification. The design is updated instantly.

• Note that the same drag-and-drop capabilities are also contained in the *Intent Manager* for 2D sketches, as was illustrated on page 6-13.

Questions:

1. How do we control the *sketching plane* so it remains the default view angle when entering the *Sketcher* mode?

2. How do we **disable** *geometric constraints* while sketching?

3. How are *geometric constraints* applied in *Pro/ENGINEER Sketcher*?

4. How do we assure two points are ***lined up horizontally***?

5. How do we access the **Divide** command?

6. Describe the advantages and disadvantages of using the *Drag and Drop* functionality available in Pro/E.

7. Create sketches showing the steps you plan to use to create the two models shown on the next page:

Ex.1)

Ex.2)

Exercises:

1. Dimensions are in inches.

2. Dimensions are in inches. Plate thickness: 0.25

3. Dimensions are in inches.

4. Dimensions are in Millimeters. (Base thickness: 10 mm., Boss height: 20 mm.)

Notes:

Lesson 7
Symmetrical Features in Designs

SECTION A–A

ø0.75
ø0.50
ø2.50
0.25
ø3.75
ø1.50
1.50
ø1.25
ø4.00
ø3.50
1.00

OREGON INSTITUE OF TECHNOLOGY
DR. BY: CK. BY: AP. BY: SCALE   DATE: SHEET: ID CODE: DWG No:

Learning Objectives

When you have completed this lesson, you will be able to:
♦ Create Drawing Layouts from Solid Models.
♦ Understand Associative Functionality.
♦ Add Borders and Title Block in the Layout Mode
♦ Arrange and Manage 2-D Views in Drawing Mode.
♦ Create Sectioned Orthogonal Views.
♦ Display and Hide Feature Dimensions.
♦ Create Reference Dimensions.

Symmetrical Features in Designs

In parametric modeling, it is important to identify and determine the features that exist in the design. *Feature-based parametric modeling* enables us to build complex designs by working on smaller and simpler units. This approach simplifies the modeling process and allows us to concentrate on the characteristics of the design. Symmetry is an important characteristic that is often seen in designs. Symmetrical features can be easily accomplished by the assortment of tools that are available in feature-based modeling systems, such as *Pro/ENGINEER*.

The modeling technique of extruding two-dimensional sketches along a straight line to form three-dimensional features, as illustrated in the previous chapters, is an effective way to construct solid models. For designs that involve cylindrical shapes, shapes that are symmetrical about an axis, revolving two-dimensional sketches about an axis can form the needed three-dimensional features. In solid modeling, this type of feature is called a **revolved feature**.

In *Pro/ENGINEER*, besides using the **Revolve** command to create revolved features, several options are also available to handle symmetrical features. For example, we can create multiple identical copies of symmetrical features with the **Feature Pattern** command, or create mirrored images of models or 2D sections using the **Mirror** command. In this lesson, the construction and modeling techniques of these more advanced features are illustrated. We will also go over the procedure to generate 2D multi-view drawings from 3D solid models.

Drawings from Parts and Associative Functionality

With the software/hardware improvements in solid modeling, the importance of two-dimensional drawings is decreasing. Drafting is considered one of the downstream applications of using solid models. In many production facilities, the solid models are used to generate machine tool paths for *computer numerical control* (CNC) machine tools. The solid models are also used in *rapid prototyping* to create 3D physical models out of plastic resins, powdered metal, etc. Ideally, the solid model database should be used directly to generate the final product. However, the majority of applications in most production facilities still require the use of two-dimensional drawings. Using the solid model as the starting point for the design, the solid modeling tools can easily create all the necessary two-dimensional views. In this sense, the solid modeling tools are making the process of creating two-dimensional drawings more efficient and effective.

Pro/ENGINEER provides full associative functionality in all *Pro/ENGINEER* software modules. This functionality allows us to change the design at any level, and the system reflects it at all levels automatically. For example, the solid model can be modified in the standard *Part Modeler* and the system automatically reflects that change in the *Drawing* layout. And we can also modify a feature dimension in the *Drawing* layout, and the system automatically updates the solid model in all applications.

A Revolved Design: *Wheel*

❖ Based on your knowledge of *Pro/ENGINEER*, how many features would you use to create the design? Which feature would you choose as the **base feature** of the model? Identify the symmetrical features in the design and consider other possibilities in creating the design. You are encouraged to create the model on your own prior to following through the tutorial.

1. Select the **Pro/ENGINEER** icon at the desktop or type [*proe*] at your system prompt to start *Pro/ENGINEER*. The *Pro/ENGINEER* main window will appear on the screen.

2. Pick the **New Object** icon in the toolbar. (We can also use the key combination **Ctrl-N** to start a new object.)

3. In the *New* form, enter **Wheel** as the part file **Name**.

4. Accept the use of the default template, which sets up the *system units* to **Inch Pound Second**. Pick **OK** to continue.

Modeling Strategy - A Revolved Design

Creating the Base Feature

1. In the Menu Manager window, select

   Feature → Create → Solid → Protrusion

2. In the **SOLID OPTS** submenu, select

   Revolve → Solid → Done

3. In the **ATTRIBUTES** submenu, select

   One Side → Done

4. On your own, set up datum plane **FRONT** as the *sketching plane* and use the datum plane **RIGHT** as the *reference plane* to face toward the **right** side of the computer screen.

2D Sketching

1. Proceed to accept the default selection of the two datum planes, **Right** and **Top,** as the references for the 2D sketch.

2. In the *Sketcher* toolbar, select
    Create Centerline.

3. Create a horizontal line by first selecting a point on the horizontal axis (**TOP**).

4. Select a second point aligned to datum plane **TOP** to create a horizontal centerline.

5. Next, switch to sketching regular line entities. In the *Sketcher* toolbar, select **Line**.

6. On your own, create a closed region sketch approximate in shape as shown below. At this point, concentrate on the **shape** and **form** of the design. The dimension values may appear differently on your screen. Note there is no *equal length* constraint in the sketch.

❖ Note that the wheel design is symmetrical about a horizontal axis as well as a vertical axis, which allows us to simplify the 2D sketch as shown.

Creating Diameter Dimensions

➢ *Pro/ENGINEER* provides a special option to create dimensions that will account for the symmetrical nature of the design; this is known as the ***diameter dimension***. **To create a diameter dimension: pick the entity, pick the centerline to use as the axis of revolution, and pick the entity again; then place the dimension.**

1. Select **Dimension** in the *Sketcher* toolbar.

2. & 4. Pick this line

5. Place the text

3. Pick the centerline

2. Pick the top horizontal line as the first entity to dimension.

3. Pick the horizontal centerline.

4. Pick the top horizontal line again.

5. Pick a location, with the middle-mouse-button, toward the right side of the sketch as shown.

❖ The diameter dimension uses the centerline as a reference to calculate the dimension value.

6. On your own, repeat the above steps and create additional dimensions as shown.

❖ Notice many of the *weak* dimensions were removed by the system as we created the desired dimensions.

Modify the Values of Dimensions

1. Choose **Select** in the *Sketcher* toolbar.

2. Select dimensions by enclosing all of the dimension text inside a *selection window*. (Use the left-mouse-button to drag inside the graphics area.)

3. Choose **Modify Dimension** in the *Sketcher* toolbar.

4. In the *Modify Dimensions* window, toggle *off* the **Regenerate** option by left-clicking once on the option.

5. On your own, modify the dimension values so that they appear as shown in the figure.

6. Click the **Accept** button to regenerate the sketch and exit the *Modify Dimensions* dialogue box.

7. Click on the **Accept** icon to accept the completed section.

Completing the Revolved Feature

❖ For the **Revolve** operation, the 2D section needs to be a valid *section* (no self-intersecting edges), and the axis selected cannot cause the resultant model to intersect with itself. The axis of rotation can be one of the edges, but the axis cannot go through the middle of the *section*.

1. In the **Rev To** submenu, pick **360** for the revolve angle.

2. Pick **Done** to continue.

3. Pick **Preview** in the feature dialogue box to examine the solid feature.

4. Use the *Dynamic Viewing* function ([Ctrl] + [middle mouse button]) to view the 3D model.

5. Pick **OK** in the feature dialogue box to create the solid feature.

Using the Mirror Option

- In *Pro/ENGINEER*, features can be mirrored to create and maintain complex symmetrical features. We can mirror a feature about a datum plane or a specified surface. We can create a mirrored feature while maintaining the original parametric definitions, which can be quite useful in creating symmetrical features. For example, we can create one quadrant of a feature, then mirror it twice to create a solid with four identical quadrants.

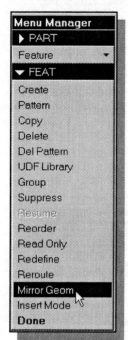

1. In the **Menu Manager** window, select

Feature → Mirror Geom

2. In the message area, the message *"Select a plane or create a datum to mirror about"* is displayed. Pick datum plane **RIGHT**, in the *Model Tree* window, as the plane about which to mirror.

❖ All previously defined features, including datum planes, are duplicated and merged together.

➢ Now is a good time to save the model (Quick key: [Ctrl] + [S]). It is a good habit to save your model periodically, just in case something might go wrong while you are working on the model. You should also save the model after you have completed any major constructions.

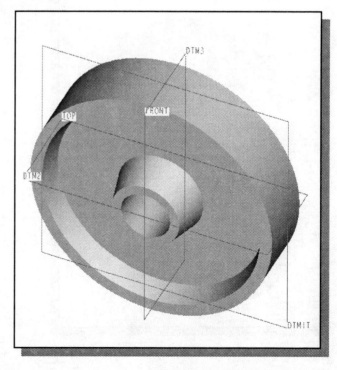

Adding a Radial Hole Feature

❖ We will create a circular hole as the next solid feature, which will be used as a *pattern leader* for the subsequent pattern feature.

1. In the **Menu Manager** window, select

   Feature → Create → Solid → Hole

   ❖ The *Placed Hole* dialog box appears on the screen. We will set up the required elements in the different sections displayed.

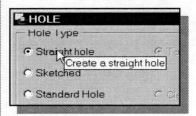

2. In the **Hole Type** section option, set the type to: **Straight hole**.

3. In the **Hole Dimension** section, enter **1.5** as the hole **Diameter**. Set the **Depth One** option to **Thru All** and the **Depth Two** option to **Thru All** as shown in the figure below. (Note the corresponding direction symbols shown in the display area.)

4. In the **Hole Placement** section, select datum plane **RIGHT** (pick in the *Model Tree* window) as the *primary reference*.

5. For the *axial reference*, select the axis that passes through the center of the model (**A_1**) and enter **3.0** as the distance (press the **ENTER** key once.)

6. For the *angular reference*, select datum plane **FRONT** (pick in the *Model Tree* window) and set the Angle to **0.0**, which will align to the datum plane **FRONT**. (Press the **ENTER** key once to accept the new value.)

7. Pick **OK** in the feature dialogue box to create the placed hole feature.

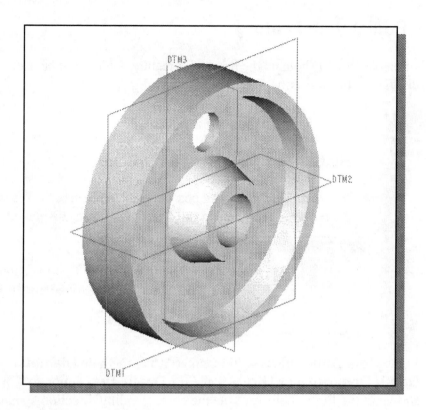

Create a Circular Pattern

1. In the **FEATURE** menu, select **Pattern**.

2. Pick the *hole* feature we just created.

3. In the **PAT OPTIONS** submenu, select

    Identical → Done

4. In the **PAT DIM INCR** submenu, select **Value**.

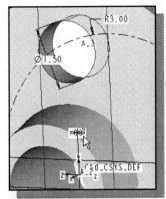

5. Pick the angle dimension (**0.0**).

6. Enter **72** in the message area as the *increment dimension*.

7. Pick **Done** in the **EXIT** submenu.

8. Enter **5** in the message area for the **Total Number Of Instances**.

9. Pick **Done** in the **EXIT** submenu.

Parametric Relations

1. In the **PART** menu, select **Relations**.

In part files, we can establish three types of **parametric relations**:

*   **Part Relations** relate different feature parameters to each other in a single model.

*   **Feature Relations** relate specific parameters within one feature in the model. A feature relation can be for the 2D sketch only or for the entire feature.

*   **Pattern Relations** relate specific parameters within a pattern in the model.

*   In this lesson, we will demonstrate the use of part relations by creating relations using parameters from different features.

2. In the display area, pick the second hole in the pattern. (The second hole's center axis is labeled **A_4**.)

3. Take note of the dimension labels for the angular dimension between holes (**d12**), the number of holes (**P13**), and the radius for the center location of pattern (**d10**). The labels might appear differently on your screen. Use the *Dynamic Rotation* function to get a better view of the dimensions.

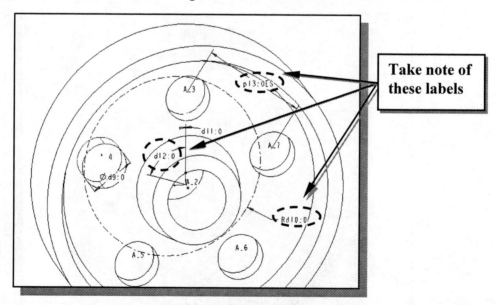

4. Press and hold down the [Ctrl] key and press the [R] key once. This is the quick-key combination to **Repaint** the display area.

5. Pick the main body of the ***Wheel***. Take note of the outer edge radii, **d0** and **d1** in the below figure.

6. In the **RELATIONS** submenu, pick **Add**.

7. In the message area, enter the following relations (use the corresponding variable names you wrote down):

    /* Rim diameter
    d1=d0*9/10
    /* Angular dimension between holes
    d12=360/p13
    /* Pattern Radius
    d10=d0*6/20

8. Pick **Done** in the **MODEL REL** submenu.

9. In the **PART** menu, pick **Modify**.

10. Pick the main body of the *Wheel* and change the *overall radius* (**d0**) to **10.5**.

11. Pick any of the holes to display associated dimensions and change the *number of holes* to **6**.

12. Pick **Done** in the **Modify** submenu.

13. Pick **Regenerate** in the **PART** menu.

• The design is updated while the system maintains the relations entered.

14. Pick the main body of the *Wheel* and change the overall radius (**d0**) back to **10**.

15. Pick **Done** in the **Modify** submenu.

16. Pick **Regenerate** in the **PART** menu.

Saving the Part

• On your own, **Save** the model by selecting the **File** pull-down menu from the icon panel. Notice that you can also use the **Ctrl-S** combination (pressing down the [Ctrl] key and hit the [S] key once) to save the part.

Creating a Multi-View Part Drawing

➤ *Pro/ENGINEER* allows us to generate 2D engineering drawings from solid models so that we can plot the drawings to any exact scale on paper. An engineering drawing is a tool that can be used to communicate engineering ideas/designs to manufacturing, purchasing, service, and other departments. Until now we have been working in *Part Modeling* mode to create our design in ***full size***. We can arrange our design on a two-dimensional sheet of paper so that the plotted hardcopy is exactly what we want. This two-dimensional sheet of paper is known as the *Drawing* mode in *Pro/ENGINEER*. In general, each company uses a set of standards for drawing content, based on the type of product and also on established internal processes. The appearance of an engineering drawing varies depending on when, where, and for what it is produced. However, the general procedure for creating an engineering drawing from a solid model is fairly well defined. In *Pro/ENGINEER*, creation of 2D engineering drawings from solid models consists of four basic steps: drawing sheet formatting, creating/positioning views, annotations, and printing/plotting.

1. Pick the **New Object** icon in the toolbar. (We can also use the key combination **Ctrl-N** to start a new object.)

Pick **Create New Object**

2. In the *New* form, select **Drawing** under the **Type** list.

3. Enter **Wheel** as the drawing file **Name**.

4. Toggle *off* the **Use default template** option.

5. Pick **OK** to start a new drawing file.

6. In the *New Drawing* form, the currently active part is automatically selected as the drawing model.

7. Confirm the **Specify Template** option is set to **Empty** and the **Orientation** option is set to **Landscape**.

8. Pick **B** size (11" X 17") in the **Standard Size** list.

9. Pick **OK** to proceed with the drawing layout.

❖ A new window will appear with the title "**WHEEL**." Notice the icon at the top-left corner of the window indicating the file type. The part window is pushed into the background and can be made active at any time.

Adding the Primary Base View

❖ In *Pro/ENGINEER Drawing* mode, the first drawing view we create is called a **base view**. A *base view* is the primary view in the drawing; other views can be derived from this view. When creating a *base view*, *Pro/ENGINEER* allows us to specify the view to be shown. *Pro/ENGINEER* allows us to select any view to be used as the base view. Note that there can be more than one *base view* in a drawing.

1. In the **DRAWING** menu, select

   Views → Add View

2. In the **Add View** submenu, pick **Done** to accept the default settings.

   General → Full View → No Xsec →
   No Scale → Done

3. The message "*Select CENTER POINT for drawing view*" is displayed in the message area. Pick a point that is about one-fourth to the left of the center of the window. The default view of the model is positioned in the display window and a drawing scale is set automatically.

4. Next we will set the orientation of the primary view. Pick **DTM1** or datum plane **RIGHT** in the display area.

5. In the display area, pick **DTM2** or datum plane **TOP** to face the *top* edge of the screen.

6. Pick **OK** to accept the orientation of the primary base view.

Adding a Projected Sectional View

❖ To create a section view, a view projection line is required. The **view projection line**, also known as the **cutting plane line**, defines a cutting line for the section view. Depending upon how a view projection line is drawn, the line can be used to define the type of section view or define a boundary for a partial view. If the view projection line is created outside the base view, it defines a plane from which to project an auxiliary view.

1. In the **DRAWING** menu, select

    VIEWS → Add View

2. In the **Add View** submenu, select

    Projection → Full View → Section → No Scale → Done

❖ We will add a right side full section view; *Pro/ENGINEER* will orient this view to be a projection of the primary front view.

3. In the **XSEC TYPE** submenu, select

   Full → Total Xsec → Done

4. The message "*Select CENTER POINT for drawing view*" is displayed in the message area. Pick a point that is to the right of the primary view in the display area.

5. In the **XSEC ENTER** submenu, select

   Create → Planar → Single → Done

6. In the message area, enter **A** as the **Name For The Cross-Section**.

7. Pick datum plane **FRONT** in the front view to establish a vertical line through the **Wheel**.

8. Pick the *primary base view* (front view) to place the cutting plane line and arrows.

9. Pick **Done/Return** to exit the **VIEWS** submenu.

Modify the Overall Drawing Display

1. Select the **Display Datum Plane On/Off** icon in the toolbar to toggle *off* the display of the datum planes. Notice the other **Display** icons are located next to this icon. On your own, toggle *off* the display of axes and coordinate system.

Display Datum Plane control icon

2. Press and hold down the [Ctrl] key and press the [R] key once. This is the quick-key combination to **Repaint** the display area.

3. In the **Pull-down** menu, pick **Edit**.

4. Pick **Value** in the Edit pull-down menu list.

5. Move the cursor to the bottom of the display area. Left-click once on **SCALE**.

Pick *SCALE*

Enter *0.5*

6. In the message area, enter **0.5** as the new scale factor.

7. In the **Menu Manager** menu, pick **Views → Move View**.

8. Pick the views and drag with the left-mouse-button to reposition the views as shown.

9. Click **Done/Return** in the **Views** submenu to end the Move Views command.

10. Click on the upper arrow to select the entity.

11. Reposition the location of the selected arrow by dragging the arrow with the left-mouse-button.

12. Pick the letter **A**, next to the arrow, with the left-mouse-button.

13. Drag and drop with the left-mouse-button to reposition the label.

14. On your own, repeat the above steps and reposition the arrows and text as shown.

Adjusting the Display Mode of Views

1. In the **DRAWING** menu, select

   Views → Disp Mode → View Disp

2. Pick both views.

3. Pick **Done Sel** in the **GET SELECT** submenu.

4. In the **View Disp** submenu, select

   **No Hidden → Tan Default →
   Hide Skeleton → Drawing Color
   → Done**

5. Pick **Done/Return** in the **VIEWS** submenu.

SECTION A-A

Displaying Feature Dimensions

- By default, feature dimensions are not displayed in 2D views in *Pro/ENGINEER*. We can change the default settings while creating the views or switch on the display of the parametric dimensions using the **Show/Erase** option menu.

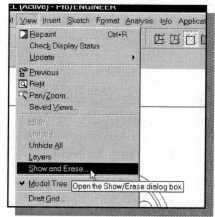

1. In the **View** pull-down menu, select **Show and Erase.**

2. Pick the **Regular Dimension** icon in the *Show/Erase* form.

3. In the **Show By** list, select **Feat_View**.

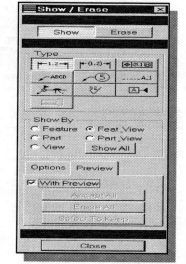

4. In the **Preview** option list, toggle *on* the **With Preview** option.

5. In the message area, the message "*Select a feature in the picked view.*" is displayed. Pick the main body feature in the section view.

6. Pick **Done Sel** in the **GET SELECT** submenu.

SECTION A-A

7. In the *Show/Erase* form, the **Select to Remove** option is highlighted. Pick the unwanted dimensions displayed in the section view. Notice the different **Unsel** options that are available in the **GET SELECT** menu. (The repositioning of dimensions is illustrated in the following sections.)

8. Pick **Done Sel** to accept the selection.

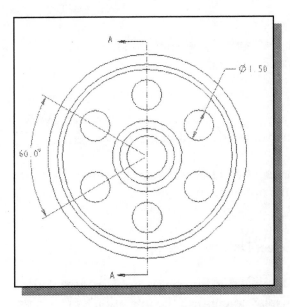

9. Pick the **hole pattern** in the *front view* and, on your own, remove any unwanted dimensions.

10. Pick the **Close** button in the *Show/Erase* form to exit the Show and Erase command.

Adding/Deleting Additional Dimensions – Driven Dimensions

❖ Besides displaying the **feature dimensions**, dimensions used to create the features, we can also add additional **driven dimensions** to the drawing. *Feature dimensions* are used to control the geometry, where *driven dimensions* are controlled by the existing geometry. In the drawing layout, we can therefore **delete** the *driven dimensions* but we can only **hide** the *feature dimensions*. One should try to use as many *feature dimensions* as possible and add *driven dimensions* only if necessary. It is also more effective to use *feature dimensions* in the drawing layout since they are created when the model was built.

1. In the **Insert** pull-down menu, select **Dimension → New References**

2. In the **Attach Type** submenu, confirm the selection of **On Entity → Pick**.

❖ Note that we add dimensions the same way we did in the *2D Sketcher*.

3. Pick the two inside vertical edges and create the dimension as shown.

Create this dimension.

4. Pick **Return** in the **Attach Type** submenu to exit the **Insert Dimension** command.

5. Pick the driven dimension we added in the above steps.

6. Inside the display area, click once with the right-mouse-button to bring up the option menu.

7. Select **Delete** in the option list.

8. Deselect the dimension and **Repaint** the display to confirm the operation.

*   In the *Pro/ENGINEER Drawing mode*, the **Delete** option is used to remove entities from the database. The **Erase** option is used to temporarily remove the highlighted entity from the display. *Feature dimensions* can only be *erased*, not *deleted* from the drawing, through the **Show/Erase** option.

9. On your own, repeat the above steps and create the desired dimensions in the 2D views.

Dimension Appearances

1. Exit any command and confirm the **Select** option is active.

2. Pick one of the dimensions to move. Several small markers appear on the selected dimension.

3. Move the cursor on top of the small markers and note the cursor indicates the direction that can be moved.

4. Use the left-mouse-button to drag one of the markers to reposition the text and/or dimension lines, as well as the arrowheads.

5. Pick a new location to place the dimension.

6. On your own, repeat the above steps and reposition the displayed dimensions.

7. Pick the driven dimension we added in the above steps.

8. Inside the display area, click once with the right-mouse-button to bring up the option menu.

9. Select **Flip Arrows** in the option list.

• Notice the directions of the arrows are flipped as shown.

10. Pick the dimension text of the center hole (diameter 2.0) in the section view as shown.

11. Inside the display area, click once with the right-mouse-button to bring up the option menu.

12. Select **Switch View** in the option list.

13. The message "*Select model view or window*" is displayed in the message area. Pick the primary view, the **Front** view, in the display area.

• The dimension is moved to the front view.

14. On your own, adjust the dimensions so that they appeared as shown in the figure below.

Displaying Centerlines

1. In the **View** pull-down menu, select **Show and Erase.**

2. Pick the **Axis** icon in the *Show/Erase* form.

3. On your own, toggle *off* any other types of dimension details under the **Type** list.

4. In the **Show By** list, select **View.**

5. In the **Preview** option list, toggle *on* the **With Preview** option.

6. In the message area, the message "*Select model view or window.*" is displayed. Pick the section view.

SECTION A-A

7. In the *Show/Erase* form, set the **Select to Keep** option. Keep only the three centerlines to be displayed in the section view as shown.

8. Pick **Done Sel** to accept the selection. Notice the **Unsel** options available in the **Get Select** menu.

9. Repeat the same procedure to display centerlines in the front view.

10. Pick the **Close** button in the *Show/Erase* form to exit the Show/Erase command.

11. In the **View** pull-down menu, select **Display Settings → Datum Display**

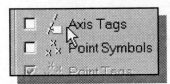

12. In the *Datum display* dialogue box, switch *off* the **Axis Tags** option as shown.

13. Click **OK** to exit the *Datum display* dialogue box.

Adjusting the Length of Centerlines

1. Pick the axis that is through the center of the section view as shown.

2. Two small markers appear on the centerline. Use the left-mouse-button to drag one of the markers to lengthen/shorten the centerline.

3. On your own, repeat the above steps and adjust the length of the displayed centerlines.

❖ Note that the same procedure is used to adjust the location of any dimensions as well as the size of dimension related entities.

Creating Additional Centerlines

1. In the *Sketch* Toolbar, select the **Circle** command.

• Note that the *Sketch* option allows us to create 2D entities that exist only in *Drawing mode*.

2. Click on the **Arrow** icon to activate the selection of *Snapping References* as shown.

3. Select the center circle as a *Snapping Reference* as shown.

4. Pick **Done Sel** in the **GET SELECT** submenu.

5. Pick the center point of the snapping reference we just identified.

6. Press down the right-mouse-button to bring up the option menu.

7. Select **Specify Radius** as shown.

8. Enter **1.5** as the radius of the circle as shown. (Why 1.5?)

9. Inside the display area, click once with the middle-mouse-button to end the Sketch Circle command.

10. Select the circle we just created.

11. Inside the display area, click once with the right-mouse-button to bring up the option menu

12. Select **Properties** in the option list as shown.

13. Set the Line Font to **CTRLFON_L_L** as shown.

14. Click on the **Apply** button to accept the setting.

15. Click on the **Close** button to exit the Modify Line Style option.

16. On your own, use the **Insert →
Dimension** command to create the diameter dimension of the circle as shown. (Hint: Double-click on the circle to switch from radius to diameter.)

• The drawing is set to half scale and the size of the created circle reflects that.

17. In the **Menu Manager**, select:

Advanced → Draw Setup

18. Scroll down the option list and set the **draft_scale** option to **0.5**, matching the drawing scale we set on page 7-21.

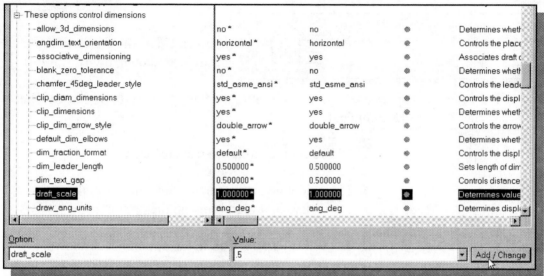

19. Click on the **Add/Change** button as shown in the figure above.

20. Click on the **Apply** button to accept the settings.

21. Click on the **Close** button to exit the Draw Setup command.

22. In the Menu Manager, click **Done/Return** to exit the **Advanced** submenu.

23. In the Menu Manager, select:
    Regenerate → Draft

• The dimension for the centerline circle has been updated to reflect the drawing scale used.

Associative Functionality – Modifying Feature Dimensions

❖ *Pro/ENGINEER's associative functionality* allows us to change the design at any level, and the system reflects the change at all levels automatically.

1. In the **Pull-down** menu, pick **Edit**.

2. Pick **Value** in the **Edit** pull-down menu list.

3. Pick the dimension text (**Ø 1.5**) of the hole pattern.

Modify the hole diameter

SECTION A-A

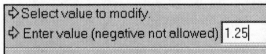

4. In the message area, enter **1.25** as the new diameter.

5. Pick **Regenerate** in the **DRAWING** menu.

6. In the **Regenerate** submenu, pick **Model** to regenerate both the model and the drawing.

7. Select **Window** in the pull-down menu.

8. Pick **WHEEL.PRT.**

❖   Notice the model is also updated as the dimension was modified in the drawing mode.

Bi-Directional Associative Functionality

1. Pick **Modify** in the **PART** menu window.

2. Pick one of the holes.

3. Pick the text of the diameter of the circle.

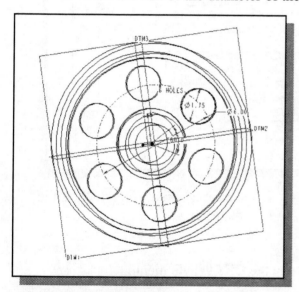

4. In the message area, enter **1.75** as the new diameter value.

5. Pick **Done** in the **Modify** menu.

6. Pick **Regenerate** in the **PART** menu window.

7. Select **Window** in the pull-down menus.

8. Pick **WHEEL.DRW:1.**

❖   Notice the drawing is updated automatically as the part was modified in the *Part Modeling* mode.

9. On your own, modify and complete the front view and section view of the design. Also, add an additional isometric view so that the completed drawing appears as shown on the next page.

Questions:

1. What does *Pro/ENGINEER's associative functionality* allow us to do?

2. What essential element is common to revolved features?

3. How do you move a view on the *drawing sheet*?

4. How do you move a dimension from one view to another?

5. What is the difference between *erasing* and *deleting* a dimension?

6. How do you reposition dimensions?

7. What are the required elements in order to generate a sectional view?

8. What is the first feature in a pattern called in *Pro/ENGINEER*?

9. What is a "radial hole" in *Pro/ENGINEER*?

10. Create sketches showing the steps you plan to use to create the two models shown on the next page:

Ex.1)

Ex.2)

Exercises: (All dimensions are in inches.)

1.

2.   Plate thickness: 0.125 inch. Hint: Create a circular disk as the base feature.

3.

4.

Lesson 8
Three Dimensional Construction Tools

Learning Objectives

When you have completed this lesson, you will be able to:
- ♦ Understand the Parent/Child relations between features.
- ♦ Create Swept Features.
- ♦ Setup Multiple Work planes.
- ♦ Create Lofted Features
- ♦ Use the Shell Command.
- ♦ Create 3-D Rounds & Fillets

Introduction

Pro/ENGINEER provides an assortment of three-dimensional construction tools to make the creation of solid models easier and more efficient. **Extrude** and **Revolve** are the two most commonly used methods, as demonstrated in the previous lessons, to create 3D models. In this next example, we will examine the procedures for using the **Sweep** feature, the **Blend** feature, the **Shell** feature, and also for creating **Rounds** and **Fillets** along edges of a solid model. These features are common characteristics of molded parts.

The **Sweep** option is defined as moving a cross-section through a path in space to form a three-dimensional object. To define a sweep in *Pro/ENGINEER*, we define two sections: the trajectory and the cross-section.

The **Blend** option is defined as joining several planar sections together at the edges, with transitional surfaces, to form a three-dimensional object. In *Pro/ENGINEER*, each planar section must have the same number of segments/vertices.

The **Shell** option is defined as hollowing out the inside of a solid, leaving a shell of specified wall thickness.

A Thin-Walled Part: *Dryer Housing*

Modeling Strategy

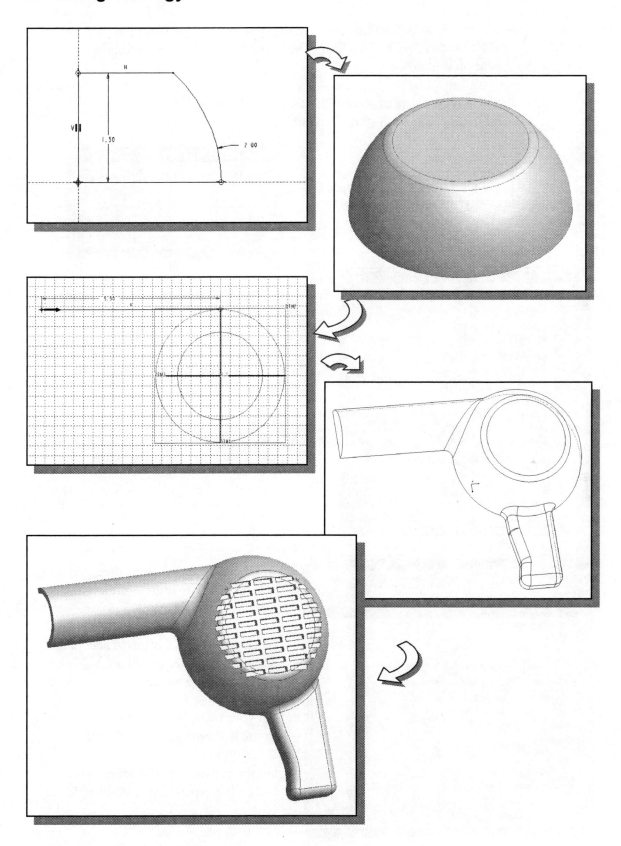

Starting *Pro/ENGINEER*

1. Select the **Pro/ENGINEER** icon at the desktop or type [*proe*] at your system prompt to start *Pro/ENGINEER*. The *Pro/ENGINEER* main window will appear on the screen.

2. Pick the **New Object** icon in the toolbar. (We can also use the key combination **Ctrl-N** to start a new object.)

2. Pick *Create New Object*

3. Enter **DryerHousing** as the part **Name** as shown in the figure.

4. Turn *off* the **Use default template** option.

5. Click on the **OK** button to accept the settings.

6. In the *New File Options* dialogue box, select **EMPTY** in the option list to not use any template file.

7. Click on the **OK** button to accept the settings and enter the *Pro/ENGINEER Part Modeling* mode.

8. On your own, set up the system units to **Inch Pound Second (IPS)**.

9. On your own, set up a set of three mutually perpendicular datum planes.

Creating the Base Feature

1. In the **Menu Manager** window, select

   Feature → Create → Solid → Protrusion

2. In the **SOLID OPTS** submenu, select

   Revolve → Solid → Done

3. In the **ATTRIBUTES** submenu, select

   One Side → Done

4. Set up datum plane DTM3 as the sketching plane and DTM1 as the **right** side reference plane.

2D Sketching

1. In the *References* dialog box, confirm DTM1 and DTM2 are selected as the references for the 2D sketch. Click the **Close** button to accept the settings.

2. In the *Sketcher* toolbar, select **Create Centerline**.

3. Create a vertical line by first selecting a point on the vertical axis (DTM1).

4. Select a second point aligned to datum plane DTM1 to create a vertical centerline.

5. On your own, create the 2D section (consisting of two horizontal lines, one vertical line, and an arc) as shown below.

Center of arc

6. Use the **Modify** command and adjust the *radius* to **2.0**, and the *vertical distance* to **1.5**.

7. Click on the **Accept** icon to accept the completed section.

Create the Revolved Part

1. In the **Rev To** submenu, pick **360** for the revolve angle.

2. Pick **Done** to continue.

3. Pick **Preview** in the feature dialogue box to examine the solid feature.

4. Pick **OK** in the feature dialogue box to create the solid feature.

5. Click on the **Saved View List** icon and choose **Default** to view the completed 3D solid feature in the direction of the preset default view.

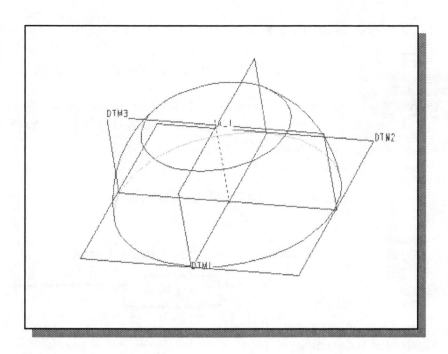

Creating a Sweep Feature

❖ A *sweep* operation is defined as moving a planar section through a path in space to form a three-dimensional object. The path of the sweep can be a straight line or a curve. The **Extrude** operation, which we have used in the previous lessons, is a specific type of sweep. The Extrude operation is also known as the *linear sweep* operation, in which the sweep control path is always a line perpendicular to the two-dimensional section. Linear sweeps of unchanging shape result in what are generally called *prismatic solids*; which means solids with a constant cross-section from end to end.

1. In the **Menu Manager** window, select

   Feature → Create → Solid → Protrusion

2. In the **SOLID OPTS** submenu, select

   Sweep → Solid → Done

Define the Sweep Trajectory

1. Pick **Sketch Traj** in the **SWEEP TRAJ** menu.

2. Set up datum plane **DTM2** as the *sketching plane* with the arrow pointing downward and **DTM1** as the **right** side *reference plane*.

3. Accept the use of **DTM1** and **DTM3** as the references for the 2D sketch.

4. In the *Sketcher* toolbar, select **Create Lines**.

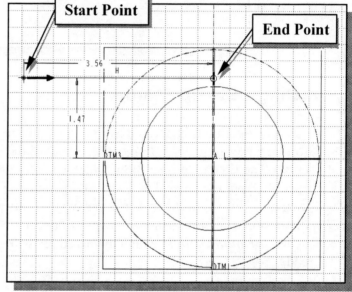

5. Select a point toward the left of the base feature as the starting point and create a horizontal line with the end point aligned to the vertical axis as shown in the figure.

6. Modify the two dimensions to **5.5** and **1.125** as shown in the figure below.

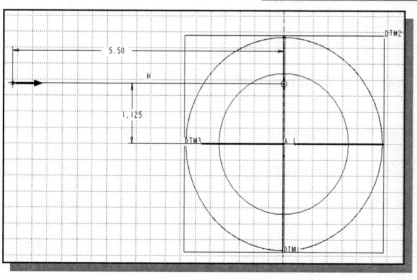

7. Click on the **Accept** icon to accept the completed *sweep trajectory*.

Define the Sweep Section

1. In the **ATTRIBUTES** submenu, select

   Free Ends → Done

2. The default references established by the system include **DTM2** and an axis that is perpendicular to the datum plane **DTM2**. Click the **Close** button to proceed without selecting additional references.

3. In the *Sketcher* toolbar, select

   Center/Ends Arc.

4. Place the center of the arc on the intersection of the two references and both ends of the arc aligned to **DTM2**.

Alignment

5. Pick **Line** in the *Sketcher* toolbar and create a line connecting the two ends of the arc.

6. Modify the radius of the arc to **0.75** so that the sketch appears as shown in the figure above.

7. Click on the **Accept** icon to accept the completed *sweep section*.

8. Pick **OK** in the feature dialogue box to create the solid feature.

9. Use the *Dynamic Viewing* function ([Ctrl] + [middle-mouse-button]) to view the 3D feature.

Create a Blend Feature

❖ A *blend* feature is a series of two-dimensional sections that are joined together at the edges with transitional surfaces to form a solid.

1. In the **Menu Manager** window, select

    Feature → Create → Solid → Protrusion

2. In the **SOLID OPTS** submenu, select

    Blend → Solid → Done

3. In the **BLEND OPTS** menu, select

    Parallel → Regular Sec → Sketch Sec → Done

4. In the **ATTRIBUTES** submenu, select

    Straight → Done

5. Set up datum plane DTM3 as the *sketching plane,* with the arrow pointing forward and DTM1 as the **right** side *reference plane.*

Creating 2D Blend Sections

1. Click the **Close** button to accept the use of DTM1 and DTM2 as the references for the 2D sketch.

2. In the *Sketcher* menu, select **Rectangle**.

3. Place the first corner of the rectangle on the horizontal axis and create a rectangle as shown.

4. Use the **Relation** option and position the rectangle centered about DTM1.

5. Use **Modify** and **Regenerate** in the *Sketcher* menu to adjust the size of the rectangle to **1.50 x .50**.

❖ We have completed the first 2D section. We will next create the second 2D section. A *blend* feature is a series of two-dimensional sections that are joined together.

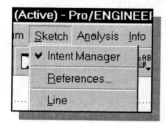

6. Select **Sketch** in the pull-down menu.

7. In the **Sketch** pull-down menu, select

Feature Tools → Section Toggle

• The color of the previously sketched rectangle turned gray signifying that *Pro/ENGINEER Sketcher* is ready to create the second 2D section.

8. In the *Sketcher* toolbar, select **Rectangle**.

9. Place the first corner of the rectangle on the horizontal axis and align the second corner as shown. The arrowhead indicates the direction of the blend. By placing the rectangle the same way as the first section, we assure that the blend will start at the same corner.

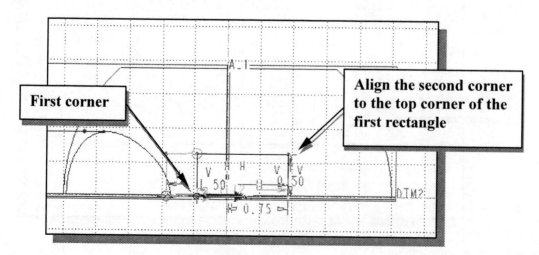

10. Modify the *width* of the second rectangle to **1.40**.

11. Inside the graphics area, press down the right-mouse-button to bring up the option menu.

12. In the popup list, select **Toggle Section.**

13. On your own, create the third rectangle (width:**1.2**) as shown.

14. Reposition all of the existing dimensions by **drag-and-drop** with the left-mouse-button.

• Note that only *one* loop per subsection is allowed for the **Blend** operation.

15. On your own, repeat the above procedure and create another rectangle (width:**1.35**) as shown. (All four sections are aligned at the top-right corner.)

16. Click on the **Accept** icon to accept the completed *sweep section*.

17. In the **DEPTH** menu, select

    Blind → Done

18. Enter **2.5** in the message area for the distance in between the first section and the second section.

19. Enter **1.0** as the distance in between the second section and the third section.

20. Enter **0.75** in the message area for the distance in between the third section and the forth section.

21. Pick **OK** in the feature dialogue box to create the solid feature.

22. Use the *Dynamic Viewing* function ([Ctrl] + [middle-mouse-button]) to view the completed 3D solid feature.

Create 3D Rounds and Fillets

1. In the Menu Manager window, select

   Feature → Create → Solid → Round

2. In the **ROUND TYPE** submenu, select

   Simple → Done

3. In the **RND SET ATTR** submenu, select

   Constant → Edge Chain → Done

4. In the **CHAIN** submenu, select

   One By One.

5. Pick the top circle, the intersection curve, and all the edges connected to the top surface of the handle; the highlighted edges shown in the figure.

❖ Note that the top-circle is actually two arcs and there are three lines along the top-left edge of the handle. (Refer to the resulting feature shown on the next page.)

6. Pick **Done** in the **CHAIN** menu.

7. Enter **0.25** as the radius of the rounds and fillets.

⇨ Specify radius value option from the menu.
⇨ Enter RADIUS or <ESC> to select option from menu. `.25`

8. Pick **Preview** in the feature dialogue box to examine the feature.

9. Pick **OK** in the feature dialogue box to create the rounds and fillets.

Creating a Shell Feature

1. In the Menu Manager window, select

   Feature → Create → Solid → Shell

2. The message "*Select one or more surfaces to remove*" is displayed in the message area. Use the *Dynamic Rotation* function to rotate the model and pick the two surfaces as shown.

Pick these two surfaces

3. Pick **Done Sel** in the **GET SELECT** menu.

4. Pick **Done Refs** in the **FEATURE REFS** menu.

5. In the message area, enter **0.125** as the wall thickness.

- Selected reference(s) will be added.
➪ Enter thickness (-1000000.0000 to 4.9829) .125

6. Pick **OK** in the feature dialogue box to create the *shell feature*.

Create a Pattern Leader

1. In the **Menu Manager** window, select

    Feature → Create → Solid → Cut

2. In the **SOLID OPTS** submenu, select

    Extrude → Solid → Done

3. In the **ATTRIBUTES** submenu, select **One Side → Done.**

4. Pick the top surface of the base feature as the *sketching plane,* with the arrow pointing towards the center of the solid model and DTM1 as the **right** side *reference plane.*

5. Click the **Close** button to accept the DTM1 and SurF4 as the references for the 2D sketch.

6. In the *Sketcher* menu, select **Rectangle.**

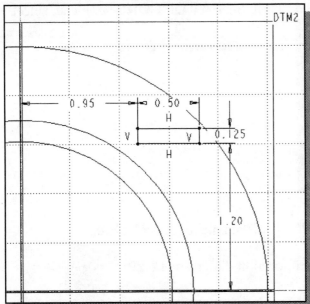

7. Create a rectangle toward the upper-right side of the solid model as shown.

8. On your own, modify the dimensions as shown in the figure. Rectangle size: **0.5 x 0.125**, location: **1.2** away from the horizontal axis and **0.95** away from the vertical axis.

9. Click on the **Accept** icon to accept the completed *sweep section.*

10. Pick **Okay** to accept the direction to remove the area (arrow points toward the center of the rectangle).

11. Select the **Blind** option in the **Spec To** menu.

12. In the message area, enter **0.13** as the *depth* of the cut.

13. Pick **OK** in the feature dialogue box to create the feature.

- Notice in the message area, the message "*WARNING: CUT is entirely outside the model; model unchanged.*" Is displayed. The other message "*CUT has been created successfully*" is also displayed signifying the feature has been created. We will duplicate this feature to form the necessary cut on the model.

Create a Rectangular Pattern

1. In the **FEATURE** menu, select **Pattern**.

2. Pick the *cut* feature we just created in the *Model Tree* window. (This feature is not visible in the graphics window.)

3. In the **PAT OPTIONS** submenu, select

   General → Done.

4. In the **PAT DIM INCR** submenu, select **Value**.

5. Pick the vertical location dimension (**1.20**).

6. In the message area, enter **-0.25** to place the copies of the feature below the pattern leader.

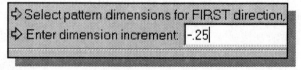

7. In the message area, the message "*Select another dimension for FIRST direction, increment type, or Done.*" is displayed. Select **Done** in the **Exit** menu since this is the only dimension that is needed in the vertical direction.

8. In the message area, enter **11** as the number of copies needed (including the original.)

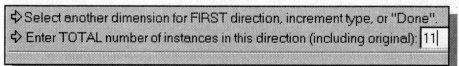

9. Pick the horizontal location dimension (**0.95**).

10. In the message area, enter **-0.60** to place the copies of the feature to the left of the pattern leader.

11. In the message area, the message "*Select another dimension for SECOND direction, increment type, or Done.*" is displayed. Select **Done** in the **EXIT** menu since this is the only dimension that is needed.

12. In the message area, enter **5** as the number of copies needed.

- *Pro/ENGINEER* will now duplicate the *cut* feature and generate the rectangular cut pattern.

Questions:

1. Describe two different methods to *modify* dimensions.

2. Keeping the *History Tree* in mind, what is the difference between *Cut with a Pattern* and *Cut Each One Individually*?

3. What are the differences between **Sweep** and **Blend**?

4. What are the differences between **sweep** and **Extrude**?

5. How do we modify the pattern parameters after the model is built?

6. Describe the elements required in creating a **Blend** feature.

7. Create sketches showing the steps you plan to use to create the model shown on the next page:

Exercise: (All dimensions are in inches.)

1. (Wall thickness: 0.125)

2.

3.

Lesson 9
Advanced Modeling Techniques

Learning Objectives

When you have completed this lesson, you will be able to:
♦ Apply the BORN techniqe.
♦ Use the CHAMFER command.
♦ Perform the Intersect - Boolean Operation.
♦ Understand the different aspects of Part Modeling.
♦ Review of Part Modeling Techniques.

Introduction

This chapter is intended to provide a summary of the basic construction techniques presented in the previous chapters. We will also demonstrate the more advanced construction techniques such as using the *Intersect-Boolean operation*, the procedure to create *drafted surfaces*, *sketched holes, chamfers,* and *complex 3D rounds*; these are common characteristics to casting and molded parts. In this lesson, we will explore some of the variations of using the basic techniques introduced in the previous chapters. We will demonstrate the use of reference geometry to construct a more complex geometry shape. Reference geometry can be thought of as user-definable datum, which is updated with the part geometry. We can create reference geometry, such as planes, lines, or points that do not already exist. Reference geometry can be used to align features or to orient parts in an assembly. In the previous lessons, most features were constructed by referencing existing features. Note that the first features we created in the previous lessons were the *default datum planes*, which are three mutually perpendicular reference planes.

Summary of Modeling Considerations

- **Design Intent** – determine the functionality of the design; select features that are central to the design.

- **Order of Features** – consider the parent/child relationships necessary for all features.

- **Dimensional and Geometric Constraints** – the way in which the constraints are applied determines how the components are updated.

- **Relations** – consider the orientation and parametric relationships required between features and in an assembly.

The *BRACKET* Design

❖ Based on your knowledge of *Pro/ENGINEER*, how many features would you use to create the design? Which feature would you choose as the **base feature** of the model? Identify the more difficult features in the design and consider the possibilities in creating the design. You are encouraged to create a similar design on your own prior to following through the tutorial.

Modeling Strategy

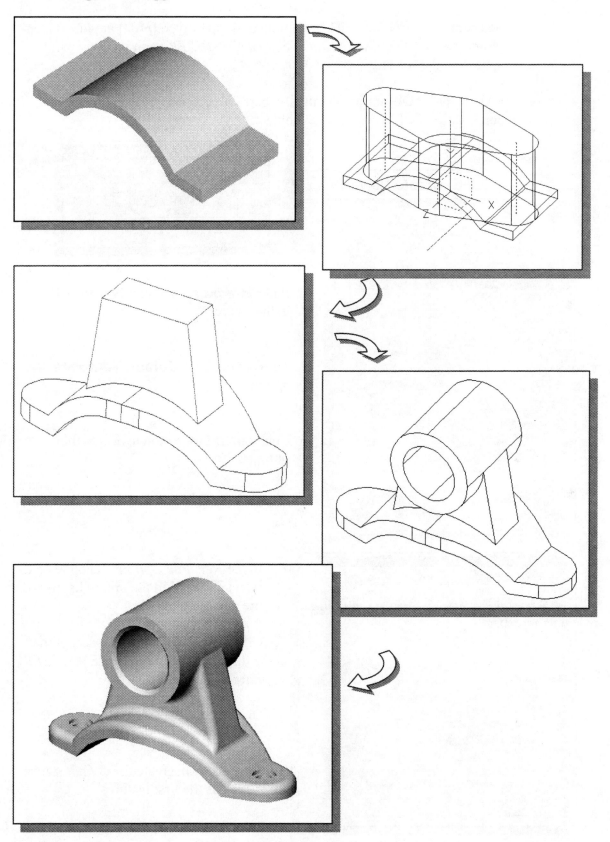

Starting *Pro/ENGINEER*

1. Select the **Pro/ENGINEER** icon at the desktop or type [*proe*] at your system prompt to start *Pro/ENGINEER*. The *Pro/ENGINEER* main window will appear on the screen.

2. Pick the **New Object** icon in the toolbar. (We can also use the key combination **Ctrl-N** to start a new object.)

2. Pick **Create New Object**

3. Enter **Bracket** as the part **Name** as shown in the figure.

4. Turn *off* the **Use Default Template** option.

5. Click on the **OK** button to accept the settings.

6. In the *New File Options* dialogue box, select **EMPTY** in the option list to not use any template file.

7. Click on the **OK** button to accept the settings and enter the *Pro/ENGINEER Part Modeling* mode.

8. On your own, set up the system units to **Inch Pound Second (IPS)**.

9. On your own, create the *default datum planes* as the first features.

Creating the Base Feature

1. In the Menu Manager window, select

    Feature → Create → Solid → Protrusion

2. In the **SOLID OPTS** submenu, select

    Extrude → Solid → Done

3. In the **ATTRIBUTES** submenu, select
    Both Sides → Done

4. On your own, set up **DTM3** as the sketching plane and **DTM1** as the **right** side reference plane.

2D Sketching

1. In the *References* dialog box, confirm DTM1 and DTM2 are selected as the references for the 2D sketch. Click the **Close** button to accept the settings.

2. Create the 2D section as shown. Note the different geometric constraints and dimensions applied to the different entities.

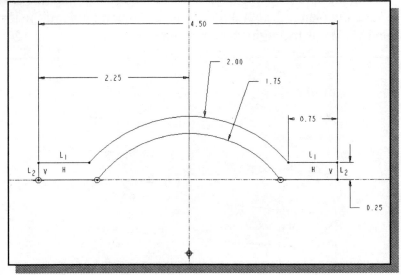

3. Complete the protrusion feature with a *depth* of extrusion of **2.0**.

Using the CUT Option to Create a *Boolean INTERSECT*

1. In the **PART** menu, select

   Feature → Create → Solid → Cut

2. In the **SOLID OPTS** submenu, select

   Extrude → Solid → Done

3. In the **ATTRIBUTES** submenu, select

   One Side → Done

4. Set up the bottom of the model, or red-side of datum plane DTM2, as the sketching plane (the cut direction needs to point toward the top of the model) and DTM1 as the **right** reference plane.

2D Sketching

1. Select the four outer edges of the base feature as additional references for the 2D sketch to be created.

1. Select the outer edges of the base feature as references.

2. In the *References* window, **DTM1**, **DTM3** and the four edges we selected are listed as references for the 2D sketch. Click the **Close** button to accept the settings

3. In the *Sketcher* toolbar, select **Circle** as shown. The default option is to create a circle by specifying the center point and a point through which the circle will pass

4. Create the three circles as shown. Note all three centers are on **DTM3** and tangent to the outer edges of the base feature. No dimension is needed for the middle circle since the center is aligned to the origin.

5. Add the four tangent lines and set the two smaller circles to be the same diameter of **1.0** as shown. (Hint: Use the *tangent* constraint)

6. Select **Dynamic Trim** in the *Sketcher* toolbar. The **Dynamic Trim** function allows us to quickly remove unwanted portions of entities by simply clicking on them.

7. On your own, modify the sketched geometry as shown in the figure below.

8. Click on the **Accept** icon to accept the completed *section*.

9. In the message area, the message "*Arrow points TOWARD area to be REMOVED. Pick Okay or Flip.*" is displayed; we are to define the ***material side*** to be removed. Pick **Flip** to adjust the arrow direction so that it points toward the outside of the sketched shape, then pick **Okay** to continue with the feature creation.

10. In the **SPEC TO** menu, select **Thru Next**.

11. Pick **Done** in the **SPEC TO** menu to continue.

12. In the feature dialogue box, select the **Preview** icon to view the resulting feature.

13. Confirm the feature is created correctly and pick **OK** to complete the feature.

Creating a Reference Plane

1. Select **Insert a Datum Plane** in the toolbar as shown.

2. Pick **Offset** in the **DATUM PLANE** menu.

Notice the available options in the **DATUM PLANE** menu:

*   **Through**: Create a datum plane through the selected object.

*   **Normal**: Create a datum plane perpendicular to the selected object.

*   **Parallel**: Create a datum plane parallel to the selected object.

*   **Offset**: Create a datum plane by specifying a distance or a specific location away from the select object.

*   **Angle**: Create a datum plane by specifying an angle relative to the selected object.

*   **Tangent**: Create a datum plane tangent to the selected object.

*   **Blend Section**: Create a datum plane through a blend section.

3. Pick **DTM2** in the *Model Tree* window.

4. Pick **Enter Value** in the **OFFSET** menu.

5. In the message area, the message "*Enter offset in the indicated direction.*" is displayed. Place the datum plane at a distance of **2.0** from DTM2.

6. Pick **Done** in the **Datum Plane** menu.

❖ Datum plane DTM4 is exactly 2.0 inches above datum plane DTM2.

Creating Another Extrude Feature

1. In the **PART** menu, select

   Feature → Create → Solid → Protrusion

2. In the **SOLID OPTS** submenu, select

   Extrude → Solid → Done

3. In the **ATTRIBUTES** submenu, select

   One Side → Done

4. Set up datum plane **DTM4** as the *sketching plane* (with the arrow pointing toward the model) and **DTM1** as the **right** reference plane.

2D Sketch on the Reference Plane

1. In the *References* window, confirm DTM1 and DTM3 are listed as references for the 2D sketch. Click the **Close** button to accept the settings

2. On your own, use the **Rectangle** command and create the rectangle (**1.5 x 0.75**) as shown.

3. Click on the **Accept** icon to accept the completed *section*.

4. Pick **Up to Surface → Done** in the **SPEC TO** menu.

5. Pick the top surface of the solid model.

Pick this surface

6. In the feature dialogue box, select the **Preview** icon to view the resulting feature.

7. Confirm the feature is created correctly and pick **OK** to complete the feature.

Using the Draft Command

1. In the **PART** menu, select

   Feature → Create → Solid → TWEAK

2. In the **TWEAK** submenu, select **Draft**.

3. In the **DRAFT OPTS** submenu, select

   Neutral Pln → Done

4. In the **ATTRIBUTES** submenu, select

    No Split → Constant → Done

5. The default option is to select individual surfaces. Pick the two smaller sides of the last extruded feature.

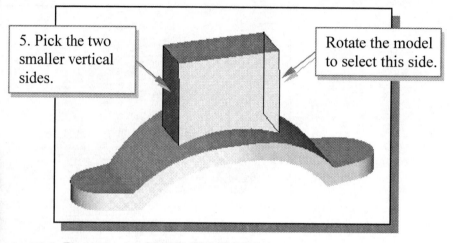

5. Pick the two smaller vertical sides.

Rotate the model to select this side.

6. Pick **Done** in the **SURF SELECT** menu.

7. Pick the top surface as the *neutral plane*.

8. Pick the top surface to determine the *draft direction*.

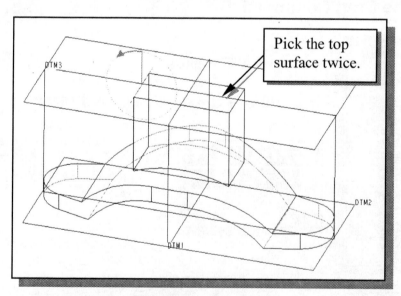

Pick the top surface twice.

9. In the message area, enter **-15** for the draft angle.

⇨ The positive angle direction is indicat
⇨ Enter draft angle [0.0000] : -15

10. In the feature dialogue box, select the **Preview** icon to view the resulting feature.

11. Confirm the feature is created correctly and pick **OK** to complete the feature.

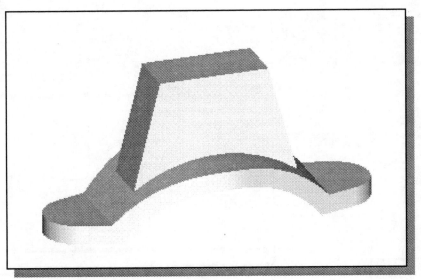

Create the Top Cylindrical Feature

1. In the **PART** menu, select

   Feature → Create → Solid → Protrusion

2. In the **SOLID OPTS** submenu, select

   Extrude → Solid → Done

3. In the **ATTRIBUTES** submenu, select

   Both Sides → Done

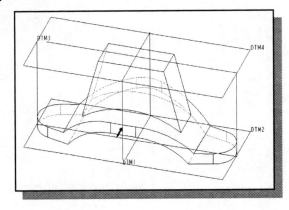

4. Set up datum plane **DTM3** as the sketching plane with the arrow pointing toward the backside of the model and **DTM1** as the **right** reference plane.

5. Select **DTM4** as a reference for the 2D sketch.

6. On your own, remove **DTM2** from the reference list. Click the **Close** button to accept the setting.

7. Create a **Circle** (diameter **1.50**) that is aligned to the two reference planes as shown.

8. Click on the **Accept** icon to accept the completed *section*.

9. Complete the cylinder (length **1.75**) using the **Blind** extrusion option. The complete model should appear as shown.

Create a Hole through the Cylinder

➤ On your own, create a **1.0** diameter hole through the cylinder we just created. The completed solid model should appear as shown in the below figure.

Create a Sketched Hole on the Base Feature

1. In the **Menu Manager** window, select

   Feature → Create → Solid → Hole

2. In the **Hole Type** section option, select **Sketched**.

➤ The *sketched hole* option allows us to create a 2D section, which is then used to revolve about an axis and form the hole. (Similar to a revolved cut feature.)

3. Create a rough sketch as shown (six regular lines and a centerline).

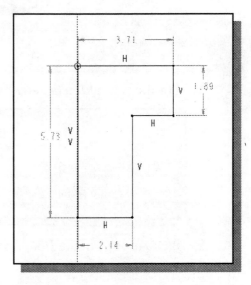

4. Create and modify the dimensions as shown in the figure below.

➢ **To dimension a diameter dimension for a revolved section: (1) pick the entity; (2) pick the centerline to use as the axis of revolution; (3) pick the entity again; then (4) place the dimension.**

5. Click on the **Accept** icon to accept the completed *section*.

6. Pick the top face of the base as shown as the *primary reference*.

Pick this face

7. For the first *linear reference*, select **DTM3** and **Align** the feature to the reference.

8. For the second *linear reference*, select **DTM1** and enter **1.75** as the distance.

9. Pick **Accept** in the *Hole* dialogue box to create the placed hole feature.

Using the Copy Function to Create a Mirror Feature

1. Pick **Copy** in the **FEATURE** menu.

2. In the **COPY FEATURE** menu, select

   Mirror → Select → Dependent → Done

3. Pick the last feature we just created.

4. In the **Select Feat** menu, pick **Done** to continue.

5. Pick **DTM1** as the *reference plane* to mirror about.

Creating Chamfers

1. In the **Menu Manager** window, select

   Feature → Create → Solid → Chamfer

2. In the **CHAM OPTS** menu, select **EDGE**.

3. In the **SCHEME** menu, pick **45 x d**.

4. In the message area, enter **1/16** as the **CHAMFER DIMENSION**.

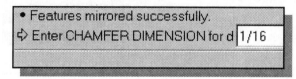

5. Pick the front and back inside circles (four arcs) as shown.

Pick these two circles.

6. Pick **Done Sel** in the **Select** menu.

7. Pick **Done Refs** in the **FEATURE REF** menu.

8. Pick **OK** in the feature dialogue box to create the feature.

Adding *Simple* Rounds and Fillets

❖ 3D rounds and fillets are complex geometric entities. It is a good practice to create rounds and fillets as the last features of the model.

1. In the **Menu Manager** window, select

   Feature → Create → Solid → Round

2. In the **ROUND TYPE** menu, select

   Simple → Done.

3. In the **RND SET ATTR** menu, select

   Constant → Edge Chain → Done

4. In the **CHAIN** menu, select

   Tangent Chain.

5. Pick the top edges of the base feature as shown below. (Refer to the completed figure on the next page.)

Pick the top connecting edges (two loops).

6. Pick **Done** in the **CHAIN** menu.

7. Enter **1/8** in the message area as the *radius*.

8. Pick **OK** in the feature dialogue box to create the feature.

Adding *Advanced* Rounds and Fillets

1. In the **Menu Manager** window, select

   Feature → Create → Solid → Round

2. In the **ROUND TYPE** menu, select

   Advanced → Done

❖ We will create multiple sets of rounds in between the four vertical surfaces.

3. In the **RND SET ATTR** menu, select

Constant → Surf-Surf → Done

4. Pick the two surfaces as shown.

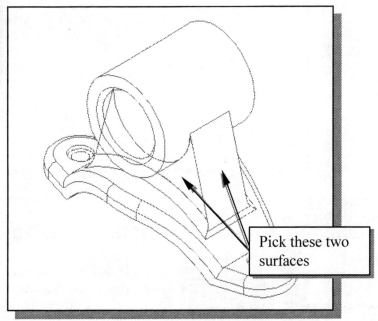

Pick these two surfaces

5. In the message area, enter **1/8** as the radius value.

6. Pick **OK** in the **Round Set 1** dialogue box.

7. In the **ROUND SETS** menu, select **Add**.

8. **Repeat steps 3 through 7** to create rounded corners for the other three edges as shown in the figure below.

9. In the **ROUND SETS** menu, select **Done Sets**.

10. Pick **OK** in the feature dialogue box to create the feature.

Adding the Last Feature

❖ The last feature will be the fillets around the cylinder. Note that 3D rounds and fillets are complex geometry and it may be necessary to create them individually, as illustrated in this example.

1. In the **Menu Manager** window, select

   Feature → Create → Solid → Round

2. In the **Round Type** menu, select

   Simple → Done.

3. In the **RND SET ATTR** menu, select

   Constant → Surf-Surf → Done

4. Rotate the model and pick the two surfaces as shown.

Pick these two surfaces

5. In the message area, enter **1/8** as the radius value.

6. Pick **OK** in the *Round* feature dialogue box to create the feature.

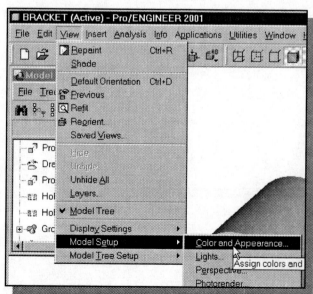

Changing Model Color

❖ In *Pro/ENGINEER*, changing model color is a two- tep procedure: (1) define the color we want, and (2) apply the color to the model.

1. Select **View** in the pull-down menus and pick

   Model Setup →
         Color Appearances

2. In the *Appearances* window, the only defined color is white. Pick the **Add** icon to define new colors.

3. In the *Appearance Editor* window, click the **Edit Color** button.

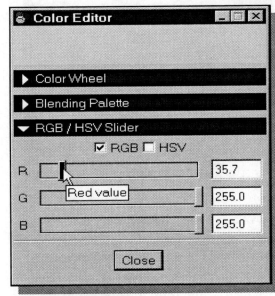

4. In the *Color Editor* window, control the amount of **red**, **green** and **blue** in the color being defined by dragging the RGB slider.

5. Pick **Close,** in the *Color Editor* window, to accept the settings.

6. In the *Appearance Editor* window, pick **OK** to accept the new color settings.

7. In the *Appearances* window, pick the **Set** icon to apply the new color to the part.

8. Pick the **Close** icon to exit the *Appearances* window.

Saving the Part

❖ From the icon panel, select the **File** pull-down menu and pick the **Save** option. Notice that you can also use the Ctrl-S combination (press down the [Ctrl] key and hit the [S] key once) to save the part. In the message window, the name of the file is displayed. Press the **ENTER** key to accept the file name, *Bracket*.

Using Drawing Format in a Part Drawing

1. Pick the **New Object** icon in the toolbar. (We can also use the key combination Ctrl-N to start a new object.)

2. In the *New* form, select **Drawing** under the **Type** list.

3. Enter *Bracket* as the drawing file **Name**.

4. Turn *off* the **Use default template** option.

5. Pick **OK** to start a new file.

6. In the *New Drawing* form, the currently active part is automatically selected as the drawing model. Pick **Empty with Format** in the **Specify Template** list. In the **Format** area, select **B.FRM** (B size format: 11" X 17"). If the format list is empty, pick the **Browse** icon to locate the format file, which is in the *FORMATS* **subdirectory** under the *Pro/ENGINEER* directory.

7. Pick **OK** to create the drawing sheet format.

❖ A new window will appear with the title "**Drawing:*Bracket*.**"

- On your own, create the necessary views and complete the multi-view part drawing.

Questions:

1. In *Pro/ENGINEER*, which command do we use to create a *mirrored feature*? Which command did we use in Chapter 7 to create a *mirrored part*? What are the differences in the two methods?

2. Will the dimension be updated when the geometry is modified?

3. Describe the *Intersect Boolean* operation.

4. How do you modify the directions of the arrows of a dimension?

5. What is the main difference between *straight* and *sketched* holes?

6. What is the difference between *coaxial* and *radii* holes?

7. When extruding, what is the difference between **Thru All** and **Until Next**?

8. Create sketches showing the steps you plan to use to create the two models shown on the next page:

Ex.1)

Ex.2)

Exercises:

1. Dimensions are in inches.

2. Dimensions are in Millimeters.

Rounds & Fillets: R 3

3. Dimensions are in inches.

4. Dimensions are in inches.

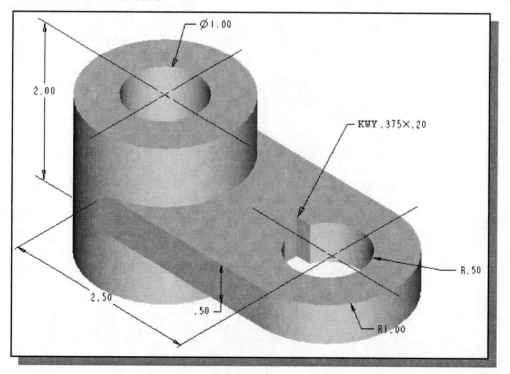

Lesson 10
Assembly Modeling - Putting It All Together

Learning Objectives

When you have completed this lesson, you will be able to:
- Understand the Assembly Modeling Methodology
- Acquire Parts in the Assembly Mode
- Understand and Utilize Assembly Constraints
- Create Subassemblies.
- Understand the Bi-directional Full Associative Functionality
- Create Exploded Assemblies

Introduction

In the previous lessons, we have gone over the fundamentals of creating basic parts and drawings. In this lesson, we will demonstrate how to create and modify assembly models. *Pro/ENGINEER* provides full associative functionality in all *Pro/ENGINEER* modules, including assemblies. When we change a part model, *Pro/ENGINEER* will automatically reflect the changes in all assemblies that use the part. We can also modify a part in an assembly. The bi-directional full associative functionality allows us to make very flexible model modifications in *Pro/ENGINEER*. Many parallels exist between assembly design and part design. The main task in creating an assembly is establishing the assembly relationships between parts. In this lesson, we will construct an assembly model using the **Bracket** part, which was created in the previous lesson.

To assemble parts into an assembly, we will need to consider the assembly relationships between parts. It is a good practice to assemble parts based on the way they would be assembled in the actual design. We should also consider breaking down the assembly into smaller subassemblies, which helps the management of parts. In *Pro/ENGINEER*, a subassembly is treated the same way as a single part during assembling.

The *BRACKET* Assembly:

Assembly Modeling Methodology

The *Pro/ENGINEER Assembly Modeler* provides tools and functions that allow us to create 3D parametric assembly models. An assembly model is a 3D model with any combination of multiple part models. *Parametric assembly constraints* can be used to control relationships between parts in an assembly model.

Pro/ENGINEER can work with any of the assembly modeling methodologies:

The Bottom Up approach

The first step in the *bottom up* assembly modeling approach is to create the individual parts. The parts are then pulled together into an assembly. This approach is typically used for smaller projects with very few team members.

The Top Down approach

The first step in the *top down* assembly modeling approach is to create the assembly model of the project. Initially, individual parts are represented by names or symbolically. The details of the individual parts are added as the project gets further along. This approach is typically used for larger projects or during the conceptual design stage. Members of the project team can then concentrate on the particular section of the project to which he/she is assigned.

The Middle Out approach

The *middle out* assembly modeling approach is a mixture of the bottom-up and top-down methods. This type of assembly model is usually constructed with most of the parts already created and additional parts are designed and created using the assembly for construction information. Some requirements are known and some standard components are used, but new designs must also be produced to meet specific objectives. This combined strategy is a very flexible approach to creating assembly models.

The different assembly modeling approaches described above can be used as guidelines to manage design projects. Keep in mind that we can start modeling our assembly using one approach and then switch to a different approach without any problems.

In this chapter, the *bottom up* assembly modeling approach is illustrated. All of the parts (components) required to form the assembly are created first. *Pro/ENGINEER's Assembly Modeling* tools allow us to create complex assemblies by using components that are created in separate part files or in the same part file. A component can be a subassembly or a single part, where features and parts can be modified at any time. The sketches and sections used to build part features can be fully or partially constrained. Partially constrained features may be adaptive, which means the size or shape of the associated parts are adjusted in an assembly when the parts are constrained to other parts. The basic concept and procedure of using the adaptive assembly approach is demonstrated in the tutorial.

Additional Parts

❖ Besides the **Bracket**, we will need three additional parts: (1)**Base Plate**,
(2)**Bushing** and (3) **Cap Screw**. Create the three parts as shown. Notice the
positions of the parts in relation to the *datum planes*.

(1) **Base Plate**

Hole sizes: Ø 0.25 and 0.6 deep.
Center to center distance of the two holes: 3.5.
Rounds: R 0.125

(2) **Bushing**

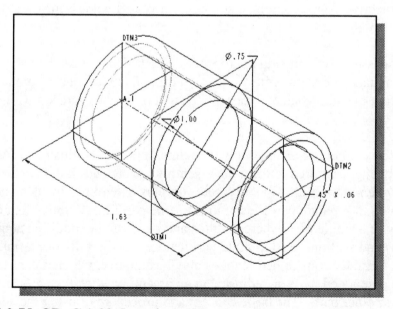

ID: Ø 0.75, OD: Ø 1.00, Length: 1.625
Chamfers: 45° X 0.0625

(3) *Cap Screw*

❖ We will omit the threads in this model. Threads are complex three-dimensional curves. You are encouraged to experiment with the tread option: **Feature → Create → Solid → Protrusion → Advanced → Helical Sweep.** Create the three parts and save the parts as separate part-files (***Base-Plate***, ***Bushing***, ***Cap-Screw***).

Create a Subassembly

❖ We are now ready to assemble the components together. We will start by assembling the **Bracket** and the **Bushing** into a subassembly.

1. Select the **Pro/ENGINEER** icon at the desktop or type [**proe**] at your system prompt to start *Pro/ENGINEER*. The *Pro/ENGINEER* main window will appear on the screen.

2. Pick the **New Object** icon in the toolbar. (We can also use the key combination **Ctrl-N** to start a new object.)

2. Pick **Create New Object**

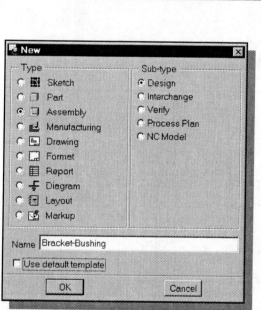

3. In the *New* form, select **Assembly** in the **Type** list.

4. Enter **Bracket-bushing** as the **Assembly** model file **Name**.

5. Turn *off* the **Use default template** option.

6. Click the **OK** button to continue. The *New File Options* window appears on the screen.

7. In the *New File Options* dialogue box, select **EMPTY** in the option list to not use any template file.

8. Click the **OK** button to accept the settings and enter the *Pro/ENGINEER Assembly Modeling* mode.

Retrieving the Bracket Component

1. Pick **Component** in the **ASSEMBLY** menu to begin placing different parts into the assembly model.

2. Pick **Assemble** in the **COMPONENT** menu. A pop-up window showing a list of part model files appears on the screen.

3. Select the ***Bracket*** (part file: *bracket.prt*) in the list window and pick **Open** to retrieve the model.

❖ The ***Bracket*** model is displayed in the display area.

Retrieving the *Bushing* Component

1. Pick **Assemble** in the **COMPONENT** menu. A pop-up window showing a list of part model files appears on the screen.

2. Select the ***Bushing*** (part file: *bushing.prt*) in the list window and pick **Open** to retrieve the model.

❖ In the display area, the ***Bushing*** is placed next to the ***Bracket*** and the *Component Placement* window appears.

❖ The default setting of *Pro/ENGINEER* will display the new component in the *Assembly* window. Note that the new component can also be displayed in a separate window by selecting the **Separate Window** option in the *Component Placement* window. Also notice the default **Placement Constraint Type** is **Automatic**.

Placement Constraints

To assemble components into an assembly, we need to establish the assembly relationships between components. It is a good practice to assemble components the way they would be assembled in the actual design. ***Placement constraints*** create a parent/child relationship that allows us to capture the design intent of the assembly. Because the component that we are placing actually becomes a child to the already assembled components, we must use caution when choosing constraint types and references to make sure they reflect the intent.

The following is a list of the most commonly used placement constraints:

- **Mate** - Selected surfaces point in opposite directions and become coplanar.

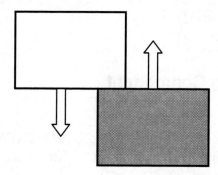

- **Mate Offset** - Selected surfaces point in opposite directions and are offset by a specified distance. We can modify the offset dimension at any time.

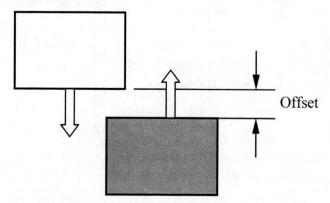

- **Align** - Selected surfaces point in the same direction and are made coplanar. We can use the **Align** constraint for axes to make them co-axial.

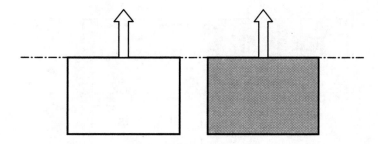

- **Align Offset** - Selected surfaces point in the same direction and are offset by a specified distance. We can modify the offset dimension at any time.

Offset

- **Insert** - Selected cylindrical surfaces become co-axial. The surfaces do not need to be full 360-degree cylinders.

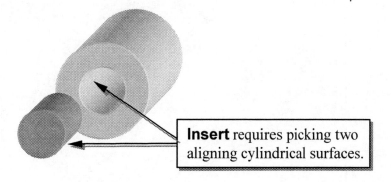

Insert requires picking two aligning cylindrical surfaces.

- **Orient** - Selected surfaces point in the same direction and are parallel. This constraint is similar to the **Align** constraint, except *Pro/ENGINEER* does not associate a specific offset value to this constraint.

Placing the *Bushing*

1. In the toolbar, switch off the display of the datum planes.

Datum plane
display *off*

Datum axis
display *off*

2. Pick **Insert** from the **Constraint Type** list in the *Component Placement* window.

Choose **Insert**

3. Pick the **outer cylindrical surface** of the *Bushing*.

Pick the outer
cylindrical surface

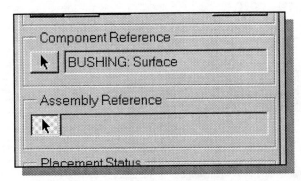

❖ Notice in the *Component Placement* window, the selected surface is identified. We can redefine the selection by clicking on the **Arrow** icon in front of the selected reference.

4. Pick the **inner cylindrical surface** of the *Bracket*.

Pick the inner cylindrical surface

❖ In the display area, the *Bushing* is moved to a new location. Use the *Dynamic Viewing* functions to confirm that the centers are aligned.

❖ At the bottom of the *Component Placement* window, *Pro/ENGINEER* indicates the status of placement of the *Bushing* as *partially constrained*. This is because the *Bushing* can still slide along the aligned axis.

❖ In general, we need to specify two or three constraints to fully assemble a component. We will add another placement constraint, the **Mate** constraint.

Create the Second Placement Constraint

1. Pick **Mate** from the **Constraint Type** list in the *Component Placement* window.

2. In the toolbar, switch *on* the display of the datum planes.

Datum plane display *on*

3. Pick **DTM1**, the *reference plane* associated with the **Bushing**, as shown in the figure below.

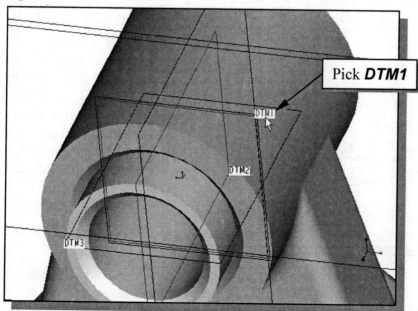

Pick **DTM1**

4. Pick **DTM3**, the *reference plane* associated with the **Bracket** part.

Pick **DTM3**

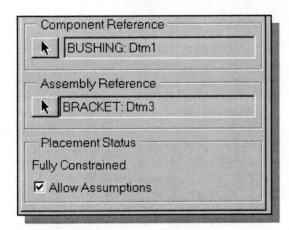

❖ In the *Component Placement* window, the components of the placement constraints are displayed. We can redefine the selection by clicking on the **Arrow** icon in front of the listed items.

At the bottom of the *Component Placement* window, *Pro/ENGINEER* indicates the status of placement of the **Bracket** as *fully constrained*.

OK

5. Pick **OK** to complete the placement of the component.

6. Pick **Save** in the toolbar.

7. Hit the **ENTER** key to accept the default filename and save the subassembly on disk.

Create the Bracket Assembly Model

1. Pick the **New Object** icon in the toolbar. (We can also use the key combination **Ctrl-N** to start a new object.)

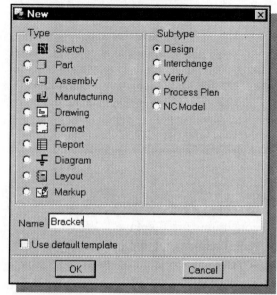

2. In the *New* form, select **Assembly** in the **Type** list.

3. Enter *Bracket* as the **Assembly** model file **Name**.

4. Turn *off* the **Use default template** option.

5. Click the **OK** button to continue.

6. In the *New File Options* dialogue box, select **EMPTY** in the option list to not use any template file.

7. Pick **OK** to continue. The **Menu Manager** appears on the screen.

- Note that we can switch to the *Bracket-Bushing subassembly* through the **Window** pull-down menu.

Base Component

❖ In creating an assembly model in *Pro/ENGINEER*, we will need to decide which part to use as the first component. In most cases, this *base component* should be one that is **not likely to be removed** from the assembly. For our project, we will use the **Base Plate** as the base component.

1. Pick **Component** in the **ASSEMBLY** menu to begin placing different parts into the assembly model.

2. Pick **Assemble** in the **COMPONENT** menu. A pop-up window showing a list of part model files appears on the screen.

3. Select the **Base Plate** (part file: *base-plate.prt*) in the list window and pick **Open** to retrieve the model.

❖ The **Base Plate** model is displayed in the display area.

Retrieving the *Bracket-Bushing* Subassembly

1. Pick **Assemble** in the **COMPONENT** menu. A pop-up window showing a list of part model files appears on the screen.

2. Select the **Bracket-Bushing** (assembly file: *bracket-bushing.asm*) in the list window and pick **OPEN** to retrieve the model.

3. Switch *on* the Show component in a separate window option and switch *off* the Show component in the same window option as shown.

❖ In the display area, the **Bracke - Bushing** subassembly appears inside a separate window, the *Component Placement* window. Placing the component in a separate window allows us to more easily re-orient the component and assembly to apply the proper constraints.

Placing the *Bracket-Bushing* Subassembly

1. In the toolbar, switch *off* the display of the datum planes and switch *on* the display of the datum axis.

Datum plane display *off*

Datum axis display *on*

2. Pick the **bottom surface** of the *Bracket*, in the component window, as shown.

Pick the bottom surface.

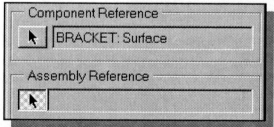

❖ Notice in the *Component Placement* window, the selected surface is identified. We can redefine the selection by clicking on the **Arrow** icon in front of the selected item.

Pick the top surface.

3. Pick the **top plane** of the *Base Plate* in the *Assembly* window.

❖ Note that in the *Component Placement* window, *Pro/ENGINEER* automatically determines the selected entities can be constrained with the **Mate** option.

4. Pick the corresponding axes, A_3 and A_1, to align the *bolt holes*.

❖ At the bottom of the *Component Placement* window, *Pro/ENGINEER* indicates the status of the placement of the **Bracket-Bushing** as *fully constrained*.

5. Pick **OK** to complete the placement of the subassembly.

Placing the Cap Screws

1. Pick **Assemble** in the **COMPONENT** menu. A pop-up window showing a list of part model files appears on the screen.

2. Select the **Cap Screw** (part file: *cap-screw.prt*) in the list window and pick **Open** to retrieve the model.

3. Pick the two *planar surfaces* as shown.

Align the two small planar surfaces

4. In the message area, enter **0** as the offset distance.

⇨ Offset (ins) in indicated direction 0

5. Pick **Insert** from the **Constraint Type** list in the *Component Placement* window.

6. Pick the cylindrical surfaces as shown.

Pick the cylindrical surfaces

❖ At the bottom of the *Component Placement* window, *Pro/ENGINEER* indicates the status of placement of the **Cap-screw** as *fully constrained*.

    7. Pick **OK** to complete the placement of the subassembly

    8. Repeat the steps and place another **Cap Screw** into the assembly.

• Note that in an assembly model, multiple copies of the same part can be placed individually using different constraints. As the assembled part is modified, all copies of the same part are updated automatically. This approach of assembly modeling is extremely flexible and effective.

Exploding the Assembly

❖ Exploded assemblies are often used in design presentations, catalogs, sales literature, and in the shop to show all of the parts of an assembly and how they fit together.

1. Select **View** in the pull-down menus and pick **Explode**.

❖ *Pro/ENGINEER* determines the default explode positions from the *component constraints*.

2. In the **ASSEMBLY** menu, select

Modify → Mod Expld → Position

3. The message "*Select an axis or straight edge as the motion reference.*" is displayed in the message area. Pick the **center axis** of the *Bushing*.

❖ Note that different types of geometry can be used as the **Motion Reference**.

4. Pick the *Bushing* part by selecting any edge of the part.

5. Move the mouse to reposition the *Bushing* part. Left-click once to accept the new location for the part.

6. Pick one of the *Cap Screws* and notice it can also be moved in the same direction as the *Bushing*.

7. Pick **OK** in the *Explode Position* window to end the command.

8. Pick **Done/Return** to exit the **Mod Explode** menu and the **ASSEM MOD** menu.

9. Select **View** in the pull-down menus and pick **Unexplode** to restore the components to the assembled status.

Associative Functionality

❖ The *associative functionality* of *Pro/ENGINEER* allows us to change the design at any level, and the system reflects the change at all levels automatically.

1. Pick the **Open** icon in the toolbar. (We can also use the key combination **Ctrl-O**.)

2. In the *Open* form, select the **Bushing** part file *(bushing.prt)* in the list window. Pick **Open** to retrieve the model.

3. On your own, modify the inside diameter to **0.5**. Confirm the part is updated before continuing to the next step.

❖ The associative functionality of *Pro/ENGINEER* assures the model is updated in all levels, including the assembly models.

4. Select **Window** in the pull-down menus and pick **Bracket-bushing.ASM**. Notice the size of the **Bushing** is updated in the subassembly.

5. Select **Window** in the pull-down menus and pick **Bracket.ASM**. Notice the size of the **Bushing** is updated in *Assembly mode* as well.

6. We will next modify the dimension value in the *Bracket Assembly* window. In the **Assembly** menu, select

   Modify → Mod Dim → Value → Pick

7. Pick any portion of the **Bushing** in the *assembly model*.

8. Pick the dimension text (**Ø 0.5**) of the inside diameter.

9. In the message area, enter **0.75** as the new diameter.

10. Pick **Done** in the **MODIFY** menu.

11. Pick **Done/Return** in the **ASSEM MOD** menu.

12. Pick **Regenerate** in the **ASSEMBLY** menu.

13. In the **PRT TO REGEN** menu, select

Select → Pick Part → Pick

14. Pick any portion of the **Bushing** in the display area.

15. Pick **Done** in the **SELECT PARTS** menu.

16. On your own, switch to the other windows and confirm that the inside diameter of the **Bushing** is updated in all models.

❖ With the full bi-directional associative functionality, when we **Save** an assembly in *Pro/ENGINEER*, any changes that we made to any of the parts in the assembly are also saved. When we save a part with any changes, the assembly is automatically updated. Consequently, we can experiment with any changes in a part without being concerned about saving the changes in the assembly. The *associative functionality* allows us greater freedom to concentrate on design while leaving the tedious tasks to *Pro/ENGINEER*.

Conclusion

Design includes all activities involved, from the original concept to the finished product. Design is the process by which products are created and modified. For many years designers sought ways to describe and analyze three-dimensional designs without building physical models. With the advancements in computer technology, the creation of parametric models on computers offers a wide range of benefits. Parametric models are easier to interpret and can be easily altered. Parametric models can be analyzed using finite element analysis software, and simulation of real-life loads can be applied to the models and the results graphically displayed. The finalized solid models can also be used directly by manufacturing equipment to manufacture the product.

Throughout this text, various modeling techniques have been presented. Mastering these techniques will enable you to create intelligent and flexible solid models. The goal is to make use of the tools provided by *Pro/ENGINEER* and to successfully capture the *design intent* of the product. In many instances, only a single approach to the modeling tasks was presented; you are encouraged to repeat all of the tutorials and develop different ways of thinking in accomplishing the same tasks. We have only scratched the surface of *Pro/ENGINEER's* functionality. The more time you spend using the system, the easier it will be to perform parametric modeling with *Pro/ENGINEER*.

Questions:

1. What is the purpose of using *placement constraints*?

2. List four of the commonly used placement constraints.

3. Describe the difference between the **MATE** placement constraint and the **MATE OFFSET** placement constraint.

4. In an assembly, can we place more than one copy of a part?

5. How should we determine the assembling order of different parts in an assembly model?

6. How do we create an exploded assembly in *Pro/ENGINEER*?

7. In *Pro/ENGINEER*, how do we adjust the locations of parts in an exploded assembly?

8. Create sketches showing the steps you plan to use to create the four parts required for the assembly shown on the next page:

Ex.1)

Ex.2)

Ex.3)

Ex.4)

Exercise:

1. **Wheel Assembly** (Create a set of detail and assembly drawings. All Dimensions are in mm.)

2. **Leveling Assembly** (Create a set of detail and assembly drawings. All Dimensions are in mm.)

(a) Base Plate

(b) **Sliding Block** (Rounds & Fillets: R3)

(c) **Lifting Block** (Rounds & Fillets: R3)

(d) **Adjusting Screw** (M10 X 1.5)

Hex Socket
flat to flat 10
depth 9

Chamfer 45° X 1

12

11

5

Ø14

Ø16

Ø10

72

Notes:

INDEX